The MARRIAGE ADVICE *I Wish I Would've Had*

What Divorce Taught me about Love and Life

GERALD ROGERS

www.epic-marriage.com
support@epic-marriage.com

Printed and bound in the United States of America

ISBN: 978-0-692-33119-4

BEFORE YOU READ THIS...

Visit **www.epic-marriage.com/intro** to download and listen to a special audio introduction I created to help you get the most out of this book.

In this free bonus audio I share some more personal aspects of my story, how this book came to be, and some important tips and insights to help you get the most out of studying and applying the principles in this book.

Thank you, and I look forward to beginning this journey with you.

Your brother,

Gerald Rogers

DEDICATION

To my former wife and to my future wife...

To my ex-wife: for the 16 years that we shared together. Thank you for all that you taught me, all that you gave to me, and all that you sacrificed for me. Thank you for standing by my side during my greatest times and through my darkest times. I can see, looking back, that I wasn't always the man you needed me to be, and I'm sorry for that. You deserved better. I will be forever grateful for your role and presence in my life, and that my children have an amazing mother like you. I want nothing but happiness for you.

To my future wife: Wherever you are, and whoever you are, I promise I will be ready for you when the time comes. I'm not perfect, and I never will be, and somehow I know you will love me in spite of that. I can't promise that I will always do all these things in this book perfectly, but I can promise that I *will* try. I will always try to cherish you, respect you, and treat you as the goddess that you are. And I will fight to be the hero, the champion, the man that you deserve.

This book, along with the rest of my life, I dedicate to you.

ACKNOWLEDGEMENTS

I need to acknowledge all those that have come into my life to encourage me, teach me, and to support me in writing this book, and all the work surrounding it. I never would have written it without the countless messages from my friends on Facebook encouraging me to do so.

My mission in writing this book, and creating the coaching programs to support people is to save over 1,000 marriages from divorce, and to empower thousands more.

I especially want to thank all those who have chosen to join me in this quest by becoming Marriage Ambassadors. These individuals have believed in me and this mission enough to buy not just one book, but a bundle to share with their family and friends. Thank you.

I know how important this work is, not just for those whose marriages we save, but also for their children and the generations that follow.

I know that I can't accomplish this without your help. Thank you for being part of my team, and thank you for being part of my life.

(For more information on how you can be part of our team as an ambassador and join us in our mission to save over 1,000 marriages from divorce, visit www.epic-marriage.com/ambassador)

{ TABLE OF CONTENTS }

Preface

To you, the reader,

Divorce was the most brutal and painful experience of my life. Many people told me that going through divorce is a lot like experiencing a death of a loved one.

For me, it was the death. A death of a future I had dreamed about, a death of a vision of growing old and walking hand in hand with this woman who I thought I would spend the rest of my life and eternity with.

When that dream was crushed, and it was clear that my marriage was about to end, it felt as though my whole life had fallen apart. With a heart that felt broken and shattered, I lost the desire to eat. I couldn't sleep and didn't want to work. I was emotionally curled up in the fetal position, trying to find meaning and hope.

My marriage of sixteen years had disintegrated.

All that remained was pain: raw and deep and real.

During those final months of my marriage before the divorce was finalized, I spent countless hours asking myself some really hard questions.

How did we end up here? What was my role in creating this? What could I have done differently? And what am I going to do different next time to make sure this never happens again when I remarry?

In looking for answers to those questions, I tried to take responsibility for my life, and poured myself into the deep work of healing. I studied about relationships through reading books on marriage and working with coaches who could help me show up differently in my life.

It was hard work, because I had to face my shadow, the part of myself I really didn't like. I had to look at myself in the mirror and see what an idiot I had been, and all the ways I had failed to show up as the man that my wife deserved. I had to look at all the things that seemed like they should be common knowledge, but somehow because of my pride and ignorance, I simply didn't know how to do in my marriage.

Through that exercise, I felt I'd found the keys that I needed to create a better relationship in the future.

Then something happened which I never could have anticipated.

It was one o'clock in the morning the night after my divorce was finalized. I was sitting in the quiet darkness of my condo, and my heart was stirring.

My four kids were sleeping quietly in their rooms, and I was thinking how different their lives were going to be from now on. I thought of my boys growing up and choosing brides of their own, and hoped that they wouldn't make the same mistakes that I had. With tears in my eyes, I thought of my precious girls and prayed that somehow they would find a man who would love and cherish them the way that they deserved.

In that moment, I knew I needed to write down what I had learned from my painful journey of divorce.

As I wrote, I imagined that I was looking into the eyes of a younger me and giving him the marriage advice I wish I would've had.

Over the next thirty to forty minutes my thoughts just flowed as I poured out my heart through the keys on my computer.

The next morning I felt inspired to share my thoughts on Facebook with the hope that perhaps maybe one or two of my friends might be inspired to show up a little more powerfully in their marriage.

There's no way I could have expected or been prepared for what was about to happen . . . .

By the end of the first day, the post had been shared over 1,000 times, and I was totally shocked. By the end of the next day it had been shared over 7,000 times. And by the end of that first week well over 70,000 people had shared it on Facebook alone.

And that was just the beginning.

It was featured in magazines, newspapers, blogs around the world, and I would have friends messaging me saying that they had just heard it talked about on the radio in Washington, D.C., Los Angeles, or across the globe in Australia.

One blog that featured my post reported that within the first couple weeks of sharing it, over 3.5 million people had come to read it on that page alone. The Huffington Post, CNN.com and many other major sites featured the article.

And then, unexpectedly, I got a call from *The Today Show*, asking if they could fly me out to New York to be featured on their program.

I was in awe. It was so humbling to see the impact that these thoughts were making in the lives of the tens of millions of people around the world who had read and shared them.

I felt this intense gratitude to God for allowing me to play this role, giving more meaning to the pain that I had gone through, and giving help and hope to others who had experienced that same pain.

During this time I received countless messages from people around the world, from Indonesia to Brazil and everywhere in between.

A lot of these messages were inspiring. People shared how my Facebook post had opened their eyes and helped them recommit to their marriages. Many couples said they had read my advice together, printed it out, and put it in a place where they would see it regularly. Some even said it had already saved their marriage.

Far too many of the messages, though, were filled with anguish, written by those expressing how they too wished they would have had this advice before their relationship had failed. And I lost track of how many women wrote me, expressing how much they'd hoped their man would show up for them this way, but that they had lost hope that he ever would.

What these messages made me realize was how united we are as humans in our desires as well as our pain.

One of the things that surprised me most was the many requests I was getting from people to write a book with more of my thoughts and insights.

At first I resisted, not feeling qualified to share, and wondering why anyone would want to listen to marriage advice from a divorced guy.

Then one day, a publisher approached me asking me to write this book, and I knew I needed to do it.

I know the words I'm writing won't be for everyone... but I thought, maybe, just maybe, there's another Gerald out there, someone who is struggling in his marriage, not sure what to do, looking desperately for hope and direction on how to change things.

I wrote this book for him . . . and for you.

My only hope is that it serves you in helping you to create the epic marriage that you desire and deserve.

With love and light, your brother,

Gerald

INTRODUCTION

Nobody gets married hoping that someday they will get divorced.

We all begin this journey of marriage dreaming of happily ever after. Yet, something happens along the way for too many of us, where we find ourselves living with someone we feel like we hardly know, not knowing how to connect, how to communicate, how to express ourselves, or how to open our hearts again. We feel distant and disconnected from the one person that we should be closest to. We feel like we are no longer lovers, but roommates, managing life the best we can. Day by day, we avoid each other and walk on eggshells, hoping not to cause any more friction.

So rather than having this amazing experience of love, intimacy, and trust, there is so much heartache in the relationship that we start to fantasize about how life would be like if we were no longer married.

Well over half the people that get married will find themselves divorced someday, and a large percentage that stay married are unhappy and feel helpless to change it.

Recently, I was interviewed on a national radio show and was asked, "Why do you think that divorce is such a problem in the U.S.?"

"Divorce *isn't* a problem," I replied.

The interviewer's shock was obvious. "What do you mean it's not a problem?"

"Divorce isn't a problem," I explained. "It is a *result*."

I continued. "I can only speak for myself, but the real problem that leads to divorce is way beneath the surface, buried deep within each individual. When we get married, we are two imperfect, flawed beings, bringing with us our own baggage, our own fears, differences in personalities and gender, and limiting belief systems that go back to when we were kids. And then these two well-meaning but imperfect people have to learn how to do life together . . . and it's not easy.

"All of these underlying differences lead to challenges with money, problems with communication, frustrations about sex, headaches and heartaches with raising kids, and different ideas and desires concerning everything else in life.

"The real problem, for many of us, is that we lack the right mindset and skillset to make marriage work. I've learned that a healthy and thriving marriage, or what I call an *EPIC marriage*, doesn't happen by accident.

An *EPIC marriage* is one where there is a deep and lasting **Emotional**, **Physical** and **Intellectual Connection** that allows there to be lasting fulfillment and intimacy.

"An *EPIC marriage* requires a mindset that includes unconditional love, commitment, trust, forgiveness, working as a team, and a willingness to choose 'in' and do the daily work of nurturing the marriage over and over again. An *EPIC marriage* requires the skills of positive communication, true intimacy, cooperation and compromise, effective money management, parenting skills and knowing how to really give and receive love."

The purpose of this book is to share some of the principles and practices to empower each of us in our relationships.

While I wrote this book as advice I wish I could have given to myself, it is for anyone who wants practical insights on how to create a better relationship.

This book is for those who just got engaged or are newlyweds and really want to know how to build the foundation for an *EPIC marriage* from the start.

This book is for those who have been married for years, have a great marriage, and want to make it better. It's for couples who have been through the ups and downs in life together and have grown stronger because of it, but always know there is room to grow.

This book is for those who find themselves struggling in their relationship, peering into the abyss of divorce, wondering how they got to this dangerous place, and wondering if there is anything they can do to bring their marriage back to life.

And finally, this is for those who have been through the pain of divorce and are now picking up the pieces of their life, looking for healing, and wanting to make important changes so that when they do enter a new relationship, they don't make the same mistakes again.

Yes. This book is for YOU.

My hope is that you will be able to read it with an open mind and a willingness to try out the concepts and exercises I share.

Our lives and our marriages won't be changed by simply reading the words in this book . . . they will be changed by living it.

Here's How to Get the Most Out of This Book:

Become a Conscious Creator

All couples struggle at times, even those with great relationships. If you are going through a rough patch now, or have in the past, that just means that you're normal. And there is always hope.

The power to change this, and to create a new possibility for the future, requires us to be, what I call, a "conscious creator."

This means for us to take 100% accountability for the results in our life, and our marriages, and to decide what we want and work toward creating it.

Drop the Victim Mentality

It's easy to point the finger of blame when things aren't working and say it's the other person's fault and think that if only they would change then things would be better. But there is no power in being the victim. If there are challenges, we need to see what our role was in creating it. That is the only way to find the power to fix or change it.

As you read this book, read it asking what you can do to improve yourself. Do not read it to find more validation for how your spouse isn't measuring up.

Reading this book with an open mind will allow you find areas in which you can improve and learn to be a better husband or wife.

Progress, Not Perfection

The purpose of this book isn't to create a long checklist of impossible expectations for you and your spouse. The point isn't to be perfect at all these things. That's not possible.

No one on the planet will ever be perfect at doing all these things all the time.

What I share here is an ideal to work toward. The point is *progress,* not *perfection* . . . getting a little better a little bit at a time.

Practice the Principles

Throughout this book, I will share some principles of marriage. There will be stories and anecdotes to deepen your understanding. And at the end of each chapter you'll find small assignments to help you practice the principles to make them part of your life.

I'm inviting you to make the commitment to do the work, perhaps sharing this journey with your spouse or some friends, and use this as a handbook for creating your own *epic marriage*.

THE JOURNEY BEGINS

December 18, 1997. How well I remember it.

It was a clear winter day, and my heart was pounding. I was dressed in a tuxedo for the first time in my life. I was nervous, scared, and excited with a thousand emotions swirling inside of me.

This was the day my life would change forever . . . and I knew it.

So much of my hopes were centered on this day. I had waited for and dreamed about it for as long as I could remember, the day where I would finally get to marry the love of my life.

I remember when I first met her. We were sophomores in college and had some art classes together that summer.

I'll never forget the first day of class. I stared as she walked in and sat beside me. She would tell you I had this dorky, glazed look in my eyes. For the next hour, all my attention was on her, not the instructor.

Over the next few weeks and months I fell deeply in love. The more I got to know her, the deeper I fell.

Here was someone who represented everything I had ever wanted in a woman . . . and more. She was fun, athletic, outdoorsy, musical, spiritual, and on top of all that, she happened to be drop-dead gorgeous as well.

We fell in love that summer, and things moved quickly. Within just a few months, I knew she was the one I wanted to spend the rest of my life with.

When I asked her to marry me in early October, I wanted it to be memorable. As we walked on campus, I stopped and turned to her. Taking her hands in mine, I knelt on both knees, explaining that it meant that I had twice the devotion of a normal man. (Yes, in case you were wondering, I have always been that cheesy.)

I told her that she was the only one I could imagine spending the rest of my life with, and I wanted her to be my wife, forever and for always.

She said yes, and as I slipped the ring onto her slender finger, I knew that I had found "my one."

And as I stood there in my tuxedo, a few months later, on that December day, anxiously waiting to see her, I dreamed of what our future would look like.

My heart skipped a little as she walked into the room. She was elegant and regal, noble and pure. And she was mine. This was MY goddess, to love and to cherish for the rest of my life.

If I were to go back in time now, and give this young, naïve groom any advice, this is what it would be…

(This is the full text of the viral Facebook post that was written the night after my divorce was finalized.)

THE MARRIAGE ADVICE I WISH I WOULD'VE HAD

Obviously, I'm not a relationship expert. But there's something about my divorce being finalized this week that gives me perspective of things I wish I would have done different… After losing a woman that I loved, and a marriage of almost 16 years, here's the advice I wish I would have had...

1) Never stop courting. Never stop dating. NEVER EVER take that woman for granted. When you asked her to marry you, you promised to be that man that would OWN HER HEART and to fiercely protect it. This is the most important and sacred treasure you will ever be entrusted with. SHE CHOSE YOU. Never forget that, and NEVER GET LAZY in your love.

2) PROTECT YOUR OWN HEART. Just as you committed to being the protector of her heart, you must guard your own with the same vigilance. Love yourself fully, love the world openly, but there is a special place in your heart where no one must enter except for your wife. Keep that space always ready to receive her and invite her in, and refuse to let anyone or anything else enter there.

3) FALL IN LOVE OVER and OVER and OVER again. You will constantly change. You're not the same people you were when you got married, and in five years you will not be the same person you are today. Change will come, and in that you have to re-choose each other everyday. SHE DOESN'T HAVE TO STAY WITH YOU, and if you don't take care of her heart, she may give that heart to someone else or seal you out completely, and you may never be able to get it back. Always fight to win her love just as you did when you were courting her.

4) ALWAYS SEE THE BEST in her. Focus only on what you love. What you focus on will expand. If you focus on what bugs you, all you will see is reasons to be bugged. If you focus on what you love, you can't help but be consumed by love. Focus to the point where you can no longer see anything but love, and you know without a doubt that you are the luckiest man on earth to be have this woman as your wife.

5) IT'S NOT YOUR JOB TO CHANGE OR FIX HER... your job is to love her as she is with no expectation of her ever changing. And if she changes, love what she becomes, whether it's what you wanted or not.

6) TAKE FULL ACCOUNTABILITY for your own emotions: It's not your wife's job to make you happy, and she CAN'T make you sad. You are responsible for finding your own happiness, and through that your joy will spill over into your relationship and your love.

7) NEVER BLAME your wife If YOU get frustrated or angry at her, it is only because it is triggering something inside of YOU. They are YOUR emotions, and your responsibility. When you feel those feelings take time to get present and to look within and understand what it is inside of YOU that is asking to be healed. You were attracted to this woman because she was the person best suited to trigger all of your childhood wounds in the most painful way so that you could heal them… when you heal yourself, you will no longer be triggered by her, and you will wonder why you ever were.

8) Allow your woman to JUST BE. When she's sad or upset, it's not your job to fix it, it's your job to HOLD HER and let her know it's ok. Let her know that you hear her, and that she's important and that you are that pillar on which she can always lean. The feminine spirit is about change and emotion and like a storm her emotions will roll in and out, and as you remain strong and unjudging she will trust you and open her soul to you… DON'T RUN-AWAY WHEN SHE'S UPSET. Stand present and strong and let her know you aren't going anywhere. Listen to what she is really saying behind the words and emotion.

9) BE SILLY… don't take yourself so damn seriously. Laugh. And make her laugh. Laughter makes everything else easier.

10) FILL HER SOUL EVERYDAY… learn her love languages and the specific ways that she feels important and validated and CHERISHED. Ask her to create a list of 10 THINGS that make her feel loved and memorize those things and make it a priority everyday to make her feel like a queen.

11) BE PRESENT. Give her not only your time, but your focus, your attention and your soul. Do whatever it takes to clear your head so that when you are with her you are fully WITH HER. Treat her as you would your most valuable client. She is.

12) BE WILLING TO TAKE HER SEXUALLY, to carry her away in the power of your masculine presence, to consume her and devour her with your strength, and to penetrate her to the deepest levels of her soul. Let her melt into her feminine softness as she knows she can trust you fully.

13) DON'T BE AN IDIOT…. And don't be afraid of being one either. You will make mistakes and so will she. Try not to make too big of mistakes, and learn from the ones you do make. You're not supposed to be perfect, just try to not be too stupid.

14) GIVE HER SPACE… The woman is so good at giving and giving, and sometimes she will need to be reminded to take time to nurture herself. Sometimes she will need to fly from your branches to go and find what feeds her soul, and if you give her that space she will come back with new songs to sing…. (okay, getting a little too poetic here, but you get the

point. Tell her to take time for herself, ESPECIALLY after you have kids. She needs that space to renew and get re-centered, and to find herself after she gets lost in serving you, the kids and the world.)

15) BE VULNERABLE… you don't have to have it all together. Be willing to share your fears and feelings, and quick to acknowledge your mistakes.

16) BE FULLY TRANSPARENT. If you want to have trust you must be willing to share EVERYTHING… Especially those things you don't want to share. It takes courage to fully love, to fully open your heart and let her in when you don't know i she will like what she finds... Part of that courage is allowing her to love you completely, your darkness as well as your light. DROP THE MASK… If you feel like you need to wear a mask around her, and show up perfect all the time, you will never experience the full dimension of what love can be.

17) NEVER STOP GROWING TOGETHER… The stagnant pond breeds malaria, the flowing stream is always fresh and cool. Atrophy is the natural process when you stop working a muscle, just as it is if you stop working on your relationship. Find common goals, dreams and visions to work towards.

18) DON'T WORRY ABOUT MONEY. Money is a game, find ways to work together as a team to win it. It never helps when teammates fight. Figure out ways to leverage both persons strength to win.

19) FORGIVE IMMEDIATELY and focus on the future rather than carrying weight from the past. Don't let your history hold you hostage. Holding onto past mistakes that either you or she makes, is like a heavy anchor to your marriage and will hold you back. FORGIVENESS IS FREEDOM. Cut the anchor loose and always choose love.

20) ALWAYS CHOOSE LOVE. ALWAYS CHOOSE LOVE. ALWAYS CHOOSE LOVE. In the end, this is the only advice you need. If this is the guiding principle through which all your choices is governed, there is nothing that will threaten the happiness of your marriage. Love will always endure.

In the end MARRIAGE isn't about Happily ever after. It's about work. And a commitment to grow together and a willingness to continually invest in creating something that can endure eternity. Through that work, the happiness will come.

Marriage is life, and it will bring ups and downs. Embracing all of the cycles and learning to learn from and love each experience will bring the strength and perspective to keep building, one brick at a time.

These are lessons I learned the hard way. These are lessons I learned too late.

But these are lessons I am learning and committed in carrying forward. Truth is, I LOVED being married, and in time, I will get married again, and when I do, I will build it with a foundation that will endure any storm and any amount of time.

If you are reading this and find wisdom in my pain, share it with those those young husbands whose hearts are still full of hope, and with those couples you may know who may have forgotten how to love. One of those men may be like I was, and in these hard-earned lessons perhaps something will awaken in him and he will learn to be the man his lady has been waiting for.

The woman that told him 'I do', and trusted her life with him, has been waiting for this man to step up.

If you are reading this and your marriage isn't what you want it to be, take 100% responsibility for YOUR PART in the marriage, regardless of where your spouse is at, and commit to applying these lessons while there is time.

MEN- THIS IS YOUR CHARGE : Commit to being an EPIC LOVER. There is no greater challenge, and no greater prize. Your woman deserves that from you.

Be the type of husband your wife can't help but brag about.

"Marriage is NOT 50-50; Divorce is 50-50. Marriage has to be 100-100. It isn't about dividing everything in half, but giving everything you've got!"

{ PRINCIPLE ONE: }

NEVER STOP COURTING

> ***Never stop courting.*** *Never stop dating. Never ever take that woman for granted. When you asked her to marry you, you promised to be the man who would* OWN HER HEART *and fiercely protect it. This is the most important and sacred treasure you will ever be entrusted with.* SHE CHOSE YOU. *Never forget that, and* NEVER GET LAZY *in your love.*

There is no magic formula in marriage. There isn't just one type of personality combination that can thrive or a single characteristic that will determine whether or not a relationship will stand the test of time. We are all unique as individuals and every marriage is different.

The most important key is a shared commitment by both husband *and* wife to make the marriage work, and you make a marriage work by doing the work of marriage.

A successful marriage doesn't just happen by accident; it is created by choice, and by remaking that choice over and over again.

A relationship is always either growing or dying.

I think when we get married, each of us wants to have an "EPIC Marriage", a thriving relationship that has **Emotional**, **Physical** and **Intellectual Connection** leading to true and lasting intimacy. We get married because this is the person with whom we most want to share our life and grow old together.

To have an EPIC marriage requires a consistent investment to keep it growing.

I can see now that consistency was something I struggled with in my marriage. There were times when I was a great husband and really focused on building and nurturing our marriage, taking my wife on dates, spending time together, expressing my love in meaningful ways, and when I did, our marriage seemed to blossom.

But there were a lot of times when I was an idiot, I took her for granted, and stopped doing many of the basics that had made the relationship strong.

I would get comfortable with where things were, and get focused on my work, or busy with the kids. I'd get distracted by other areas in life, and I stopped investing daily into my marriage. When I didn't treat it like a priority, my wife and I stopped doing our weekly date night and taking time to connect each day, and then we would drift apart.

Simply put, I got lazy.

And then when things would fall apart, I would wake up, pour my heart and soul back into the marriage, trying to fix it and work really hard until things were better… only to get lazy again and let the cycle repeat itself.

I wish I would've learned sooner that it's the little daily investments into the relationship that matter most. It's those little things that are done to make the other person feel loved that build true trust and intimacy in marriage.

Lasting love requires a daily commitment to nurture it.

Thriving, passionate relationships are created when both partners continue to invest into that relationship and make the marriage a priority in their lives long after their wedding vows are said.

When the relationship is a priority you will naturally do the things that create harmony, love, and attraction.

When you make your spouse a priority, you will naturally spend time dating, focusing on their needs, and expressing your love in meaningful ways.

When you do the basic things you did when you were courting, your love will grow, and you will experience the fruits of love, peace, and intimacy.

If you stop doing the basics, it will wither.

I think of the relationship of marriage a lot like being a garden.

We all have this fertile plot of land, filled with potential, which will yield the fruit of whatever we plant.

In order to get a healthy crop of fruit from your garden you must be willing to do the basics over and over and over again.

I have this memory from growing up in Minnesota, where each year our parents would have us kids help them plant a garden. One year, when I was about fourteen, I was charged with tilling and preparing the garden. It was hard, sweaty, backbreaking work to clear the weeds, but at last the dark, fertile soil was ready.

We had eagerly picked out the seeds we wanted to plant: tomatoes, peas, corn, pumpkins, cucumbers, and squash. As we prepared the garden, I hungrily anticipated the day when we could eat the harvest.

After carefully planting the seeds in the newly tilled earth, I watered the garden and began to wait. Each day I went out to see if the seeds were emerging yet. I watered and took care of it, and before long, sure enough, the leaves began to sprout in their neat little rows.

And then, I noticed these other leaves that were coming up in other parts of the gardens. Weeds.

At first, I valiantly defended my garden by plucking the weeds that were threatening my emerging plants, but as summer wore on I got consumed with sports, my friends and playing, and I mostly forgot about the garden. I would actually avoid going near it so I didn't have to feel the guilt about neglecting it. I knew in the back of my mind that it wasn't doing well, but I avoided really looking at it.

At the end of the summer, I was mowing the lawn near the garden and finally had the courage to look. In the place of a beautiful garden with a rich harvest of succulent vegetables, there was a ferocious crop of weeds that were taller than me. The entire garden had been taken over by these huge, nasty thistle plants with their sharp angry thorns.

If there was any fruit in the garden, it was hidden behind this unbreachable wall of weeds.

How did they get there? Where did these thistles come from? I know I didn't plant them.

How often do our relationships find themselves at this point?

You begin with this beautiful idea of how you want your marriage to be and you court and date—preparing the soil. You make the commitment and plant the seeds, and at first everything is perfect. But then after months or years of distraction and neglect you find your relationship is filled with weeds and thorns that prevent you from reaping the rewards of the harvest. All you see is what you don't want, and you want to abandon the garden, believing that what you want and deserve is somewhere else.

If we are wise, we will learn these ***Lessons from the Garden***.

Lesson 1) You must be willing to create a VISION of the garden you want to grow and fruit that you want to have. You must take the time to ask, "What type of marriage do I want to create? What do I want to experience?" And then plan how you are going to create it.

If you fail to do this, and allow the winds of nature to plant your garden with whatever seeds fall naturally, you will find it full of weeds.

In your relationship, it is crucial that you and your spouse decide together what the vision is for the future you want to have, and the types of "fruit" you want to experience, and then plan together how you can create that.

Lesson 2) You must be willing to PREPARE the soil. You cannot plant a new garden if you leave the old weeds there.

This is the deep personal work that is required to make sure your heart is ready. You cannot enter into a new relationship and expect it to be healthy if you are coming from a broken space.

Since the time we are young, weeds grow in our lives in the form of limiting beliefs, fears, insecurities, addictions and other self-sabotaging behaviors. These are the real enemies and barriers to experiencing an EPIC marriage.

The work of preparing your soil involves releasing past wounds and past attachments, allowing yourself to open your heart fully to receive that person you chose to grow this garden with.

When you notice the weeds from past wounds emerging, you need to recognize and pluck them so they don't ruin this garden.

Lesson 3) You must be willing to PLANT the right seeds. Certain fruit will never grow in certain places regardless of how much you want it to.

In marriage it's important to have realistic expectations of what you want from the other person and from the relationship. Don't expect a tomato vine to yield a pineapple and you won't be disappointed. Don't force your spouse to be someone that they are not.

The right seeds, in the right soil, cared for in the right way, however, will produce a delicious crop.

Lesson 4) You must be willing to NOURISH the plants consistently. The moment you cut the plants off from water, sun, or other nourishment is the moment the plants begin to wither and die.

The exact same is true in your relationship. If you stop doing the basics in your relationship, it too, will begin wither. Without proper care, it *will* die. It's not a matter of "if," but a matter of "when."

Unfortunately, too many then look at the withered plant they were responsible for and think it was a problem with the plant, when it was their failure to nourish it. Many then take the plant and throw it away, thinking the plant was flawed, while others stay stuck in a lifeless relationship, feeling hopeless and lonely because they don't know how to revive the sick plant.

But if you do the basics of nourishing and fertilizing your relationship on a daily basis, then it will continue to yield wonderful fruit. Even withered relationships can be revived with a renewed commitment to daily care, especially when both parties are willing to do the work of nourishing it.

Remember The Law of the Harvest: You will reap what you sow. Sow wisely.

Your current relationship harvest has come from what you have planted and the way you have taken care of your garden in the past. If you want something different, you are going to need to do something different.

Lesson 5) You must be willing to WEED regularly. If you ignore the weeds and allow them to grow, sooner or later they will take over the garden and strangle the plants you had been planning for.

This is so important in marriages. Every marriage, regardless of how rich and fertile and promising the soil was, will grow weeds. These weeds come in the form of discontentment, hurt, anger, jealousy, pride, bitterness, and fear. Even healthy couples have arguments and frustration and other weeds that creep in from time to time.

Unfortunately, when a relationship is experiencing challenges, it's easy to feed the weeds and not the plants. Whenever couples are critical of each other, they focus on each other's flaws and shortcomings, get hung up with pet peeves or grudges from the past, and consequently make the weeds in their marriage grow stronger.

Whatever you focus on expands. When your energy is on the weeds it is like you fertilize them and give them more and more power in your life, until that's all you see.

Left unchecked, any of these weeds can strangle the life out of your relationship.

Part of the commitment in marriage is to not ignore the weeds before they grow too large, but to address them when they are small and to work on healing those issues growing them... and then to do it *over* and *over* and *over* again.

The more you remove the weeds by the roots, the fewer weeds remain. But there will always be new weeds that grow. That's part of life. Problems, frustrations, and disagreements are normal. That's part of every relationship, including EPIC ones.

The great secret to a long-lasting marriage is to continue treating it with the same care when you were first courting. Keep doing what you were doing when you first fell in love and your marriage will blossom.

DOING THE WORK TO CREATE AN EPIC MARRIAGE

The purpose of this book isn't to entertain, or even just to educate. The purpose is to transform your marriage and to empower you to have the fulfilling, passionate and connected EPIC relationship you really want. That won't happen simply by reading and thinking these are good ideas. It will happen by making these principles a part of your life through *practice* in your life.

As I wrote this book, I asked myself what coaching assignments would really have made a difference to me; which ones would have helped me learn and master these principles? The result is what you have at the end of each chapter.

I've designed these small assignments as a way for you to take these principles from the pages of this book into your life. *Do them.* The goal isn't to see how fast you can make it to the end of the book. It's to make your life and marriage better, and that will only occur by taking the time to apply what you are learning.

Remember: Never get lazy in your love.

THE PRACTICE:

Commit to at least one date night a week. This should be a minimum investment in continuing to court your spouse and nurturing a healthy marriage. This is time away from the kids, and time away from any other distraction that would keep you fully present and connected with your spouse.

Brainstorm a list of 5 date ideas and have your spouse do the same. These ideas should range from fun to romantic and be as simple as a night at home to a weekend away. Then compare your list with your spouse's and figure out which types of dates you both enjoy the most, which night (or weekend) works the best, who's going to arrange for a babysitter, etc. Is one person always going to be in charge of choosing the date or will you alternate? Then prioritize which ideas you want to do first and start scheduling!

HER IDEAL DATE IDEAS

1) ______________________________

2) ______________________________

3) ______________________________

4) ______________________________

5) ______________________________

HIS IDEAL DATE IDEAS:

1) ______________________________

2) ______________________________

3) ______________________________

4) ______________________________

5) ______________________________

Here are some ideas to get your mind thinking:

FUN: Dancing, karaoke, plays, music festivals or concerts; bowling, game night with other couples, creative or goofy experiences together…

ACTIVE: Camping, hiking, horseback riding, sports, exploring outdoors, yoga, adrenaline rushes (skydiving, bungee jumping, whitewater rafting), walks in a park…

ROMANTIC: Picnics, nice restaurants, mini-honeymoons away, spa days, dancing lessons, anything involving stars or candlelight...

SIMPLE: Snuggling up to movie, giving each other a massage, reading a book together, doing a project, cooking a meal together…

RESOURCES:

(At the end of each section throughout this book I've included additional valuable resources to help you in creating an EPIC marriage. And for additional ongoing tips, ideas, tools, and support visit www.epic-marriage.com)

For a FREE list of over 60+ SPECIFIC CREATIVE, FUN and ROMANTIC DATE IDEAS as well as other tips to keep the spark in your marriage visit: www.epic-marriage.com/resources

{ PRINCIPLE TWO: }

PROTECT YOUR OWN HEART

> ***PROTECT YOUR OWN HEART.*** *Just as you committed to being the protector of her heart, you must guard your own with the same vigilance. Love yourself fully, love the world openly, but there is a special place in your heart reserved solely for your wife. Keep that space always ready to receive her and invite her in, and refuse to let anyone or anything else enter there.*

Marriage is a sacred covenant, not one that everyone is willing to make. By choosing to get married you make a promise to give yourself to your spouse heart and soul, for better or worse, for time and eternity.

In that union, the possibility arises of a lasting connection, trust, and intimacy that can come in no other way.

But along the journey of marriage there will be a lot of distractions and temptations which can sabotage and destroy that covenant.

In every marriage, there will come a time when one or both of the partners have an attraction to someone else.

This is normal.

Just because you are married, it doesn't mean that all of the sudden you are no longer human.

Especially when there is dissatisfaction in your marriage, it is easy to imagine that there is someone else who can connect with you or meet your needs better.

What you do when that happens will determine whether or not your relationship succeeds or fails.

I'm not going to sugarcoat this advice, because I've witnessed too many marriages ravaged by affairs by both husbands and wives. Whether emotional or physical in nature, the scars from affairs are the same, and the results are devastating.

If you find yourself attracted to someone who is not your spouse, STOP pursuing it!

Create the distance and the support so it is not a temptation to get closer with that person.

By nourishing your attraction to someone else and spending time building that relationship or connection, you are giving that part of your heart that you promised to your spouse to someone else.

The inevitable outcome is that you will begin to shut your spouse out more, you will seek for validation of how your spouse has failed to meet your needs and why the other relationship is right, and in the end you push away the person you have made your covenant with.

The hard thing is you can probably justify that it's an innocent connection at first, whether it's someone you work with or a friend. That person may make you feel loved or understood or important in a way that you haven't experienced in a long time in your marriage, and so it's natural to have fantasies or desires to pursue it, believing that the grass is greener on the other side.

But remember this: *The grass isn't greener on the other side; it's greener where you water it.*

We are all wired to be attracted to the forbidden, which makes that relationship all the more enticing. It may make you happy or excited or aroused, and you will probably feel validated, appreciated, and more alive because of that person, but it's all an illusion.

When you find yourself in that situation, hopefully you will have a good friend that can slap you across the face to wake you up and help you see what lies at the end of the road: distrust, disillusionment and divorce.

It's the fantasy of something that we don't have that kills our ability to appreciate what we do have.

When we are unsatisfied, it's so easy for us to seek for something else to fill that void, and believe the illusion that if we only had something else—another house, another car, another spouse, another body, another job—*then* we would be happy.

This is a great lie and a great poison.

Remember this: *As long as you think your happiness lies* outside *of you, you will never have it.*

I knew a woman who was very unhappy in her marriage for a long, long time.

She had a laundry list of complaints about her man that she had put together over their years together, and on the surface, this list seemed valid. To her, her man seemed selfish, proud, ignorant, and sometimes extremely insensitive. I am certain that this man loved her, although for a long time, he seemed unconscious of his failings in many ways. He made a lot of mistakes and didn't always know how to fix them, and to this woman, it didn't seem like he would ever change—or that he even wanted to—and so the longer they were married, the higher the walls were that she built around her heart.

Meanwhile there was this other man who had come into her life and she saw him as everything she had ever wanted. He was kind, validating, strong, sensitive, funny, and intelligent. He seemed to naturally connect with a part of her soul that her husband could no longer reach.

The more she fed these feelings, and the more time she spent with this other man, the more the fantasy grew and the more she was swept away into confusion. As her emotional affair with this other man grew, she validated herself more and more by focusing on her husband's faults and weaknesses, to the point where she could no longer see any good in the man she was married to.

Her husband fought to win her back, but by then it was too late. In time, the husband knew that he was no longer wanted, and finally gave up and left.

No one can stay forever where they are not wanted.

Truth is, despite his weaknesses, in many ways, her husband was a remarkable man. Deep, loving, strong, sincere, and loyal. After the divorce, he went on to find someone who thought he was the most amazing man on the planet, whereas this other woman was left with her illusion about her new man, which ended up not being real. This other man was married and had a wife and kids of his own, and the closer she walked toward the mirage the more she saw there was nothing there for her. She didn't realize that what she had really been wanting was in front of her the whole time. She had focused for so long on what she didn't like about her husband it had blinded her from being able to see him for who he truly was.

It's a sad story, but one that happens a lot in one form or another.

You meet someone or see someone in a movie or a book or on Facebook who represents what you really want in your life, and you begin comparing your fantasy with what you have. When you focus on what is wrong with your reality, unhappiness and frustration is the natural result.

Unhappiness and frustration can be good if they make *you* start working to become better and create new results in your life. They are good if they compel *you* to be accountable for your part in your relationship and begin to consciously create more of what you do want.

But if you see yourself as a victim, and focus only on how the other person is failing to make you happy you will be swept away into misery and believe you do not have the power to change it. You will believe that you need to go across the fence where the grass seems greener.

Happiness cannot be found by focusing on what you don't have, but only through gratitude for what you do have.

Here is one of my favorite quotes:

Be content with what you have, rejoice in the way things are. When you realize there is nothing lacking, the world belongs to you. – Lao Tzu

So guard your heart. Don't buy into the lie or chase the mirage. Focus on what you *love* most about what you have. Let that love consume you; take *full* accountability for your life, your happiness, and your part in the relationship.

Choose daily to nurture and weed the garden you do have, without looking over the fence and wishing you had someone else's garden.

If you truly want to stay together, then *focus on nurturing your love* to the exclusion of anything else. As long as you are married, give your heart *fully* and *exclusively* to your spouse, and appreciate the gifts that are in your life because of that person.

Here's the bottom line advice you should follow if you want your marriage to succeed:

If you are interacting with another member of the opposite sex in a way that you would not want your spouse to know about, it is wrong, and you must find the strength to end it, and to get as much distance as possible from that situation.

I believe you should be able to have healthy friendships and connections with members of the opposite sex, but if that line gets blurred, and you start doing or saying things that you feel the need to hide from your partner, then it will become destructive to your marriage.

So what if your spouse has been involved in an affair, whether emotional or physical?

In marriage, this is one of the hardest and most painful things to deal with. You may find yourself consumed with jealousy, bitterness, and anger. It will affect your self-esteem as you wonder why they would choose that other person over you, and it will make it difficult to trust them going forward.

For those in this situation, my advice is this: As much as possible, talk openly about the affair. Clarify the things that led to it, and learn what you can to make sure it doesn't happen again.

Here's the deal though: If you want your marriage to succeed, you must learn to *forgive* your spouse, as hard as that may seem.

Carrying that anger, jealousy, and distrust into the future will prevent you from ever having the type of intimacy in marriage you want again. And until you truly let it go, you will have those same things continue to haunt you and sabotage your relationship five or ten years down the road.

As long as both partners are committed to working on the marriage, you can find the forgiveness and healing to move forward. The affair may even end up being one of those challenges that strengthens your relationship, provided you truly learn from it.

In choosing to be married, the covenant you and your spouse made was to give each other your hearts. Protect your own heart and honor the heart of your spouse.

Be the sacred keeper of your lover's heart.

THE PRACTICE:

If you are in, or entertaining the thought of, a secret relationship outside your marriage, it is critical you end it. It's that simple. There is no way to have a healthy marriage if you are continuing any form of affair, whether emotional or physical.

The more you want to hide it, the bigger the problem really is, and the more important it is that you make the changes to end it. Of course this will be hard. You have a connection or attraction to this other person most likely because they seem to fill needs that are being unmet in your life. So as you make the commitment to end that relationship and focus your energy back on your marriage, it is critical that you identify what those needs are and find ways to get them met in a healthy way inside of your covenant to your spouse.

On a piece of paper identify any relationship or attraction you are experiencing that is distracting you from your marriage. Then evaluate that fantasy by asking yourself these questions:

What is it that attracts me to this person?

What are the needs inside of me that asking to be met?

What is stopping me from experiencing that in my marriage?

How can I create a way to fill those needs within my marriage?

What are the steps I need to take to end any relationships that are holding me back from having the marriage I desire?

YOU MAY CHOOSE TO DO THIS EXERCISE PRIVATELY, or you may choose to have an open conversation with your spouse or someone you trust about what you are experiencing and what you want to create moving forward.

RESOURCES:

If you have dealt with an affair in your marriage or are dealing with one now, you may need additional support to help you heal and move past it. There are many sensitive and personal things in your marriage that are hard to work through without the right support and mentors.

Consider working with a qualified marriage counselor, or one of our Marriage Mentors and being part of the Marriage Mastery Mentoring program.

For more details visit… www.epic-marriage.com/mentoring

{ PRINCIPLE THREE: }

Fall in Love Over and Over Again

Fall in love over and over and over again. *You will constantly change. You're not the same people you were when you got married, and in five years you will not be the same people you are today. Change will come, and you will need to re-choose each other every day.* She doesn't have to stay with you, *and if you don't take care of her heart, she may give that heart to someone else or seal you out completely, and you may never be able to get it back. Always fight to win her love just as you did when you were courting her.*

When I think back to when I first got married and who I was at the time, I barely recognize myself. I was only twenty-three, still in college, thinking I would spend my life as an artist, and completely naïve about money, marriage, and life.

I am not the same person now that I was then. I'm not even the same person I was a year ago.

So much change happens in life. Every experience and every challenge slowly reshapes us, in how we think, how we look at life, and who we are.

Marriage requires us to adapt, to grow together, and to learn to love the "new" person we are with.

It requires us to re-choose our partner over and over, and for them to re-choose us.

If you are not actively nurturing that love and appreciation for each other, it would be easy to grow apart and get to the point where you look at the person you are married to and feel like you hardly know them.

That is because *LOVE is a LIVING thing.*

Just like that plant in the garden, it is something that grows or withers based on the care we give it. And if you neglect it, there are no guarantees that your love will survive, or that your partner will continue to choose you.

LOVE is a CHOICE.

Can you choose to love someone even when it's hard?

Can you choose to love someone even when they make bad choices?

Can you choose to love someone even when their interests or opinions are different than yours?

Of course you can.

When you *choose* to love, you choose daily to nurture the love you have, and as a result that love grows.

Part of the lifelong process of choosing and growing love is to continue to be someone your partner would want to choose. This requires lifelong courting and working on being as attractive as you can make yourself for your spouse.

Take care of yourself. Dress nicely. Treat your body with respect. Eat well. Smile. Exercise often and never underestimate the value of good personal hygiene.

It sounds so obvious, but it's true. I see so many people stop taking care of themselves after they get married or have kids. It's important that you continue to work on being the best version of yourself. Too many people get lazy in this area and then wonder why their spouse isn't attracted to them anymore.

When you were dating, you were always aware of how you looked, and you tried to be your best for the other person. You were intentional in the things you did and said, and you took care of your partner. Too often though, couples get complacent after the wedding day and stop doing the basics that made them fall in love with each other in the first place.

Life will bring change. Expect that. In that change, there will be hard times and good times, and both can be fertilizer to make your relationship grow when you make the choice and effort to fall in love over and over again.

THE PRACTICE:

One of the keys to lasting love is to understand your personal "love recipe" and how it changes over time. Become aware of what you did when you were courting that made you fall in love, and see which of those things is still true today. Then define which elements of your "love recipe" are different today and what can you do to fall deeper in love.

Take time to answer these questions that describe the person you were when you were courting:

What specific things did you do that made them fall in love with you then?

In what ways did you treat them differently then than you do now?

Describe the person you need to be today to have them choose you now.

What specific things can you do to make them fall more in love with you now?

RESOURCES:

To help couples like you create lasting and meaningful breakthroughs in your marriage, we have designed a 90-day Marriage Mastery Challenge. This is an intensive three-month program designed to reignite the spark in your marriage and to arm you with the tools and support to build and nurture a healthy, lasting relationship.

Whether you have a good marriage that you want to make better, or you find yourself lingering on the edge of divorce and you want to give it one more shot, these powerful 90 days will not only transform your marriage, but also your life.

For more details and to apply visit
www.epic-marriage.com/mentoring

{ PRINCIPLE FOUR: }

ALWAYS SEE THE BEST

ALWAYS SEE THE BEST IN HER. Focus only on what you love. What you focus on will expand. If you focus on what bugs you, all you will see are reasons to be bugged. If you focus on what you love, you can't help but be consumed by love. Focus to the point where you can no longer see anything but love, and you know without a doubt that you are the luckiest man on earth to have this woman as your wife.

One of the most basic yet elusive truths in life is this: *You always see what you want to see* and *you will always find what you are looking for.*

Imagine I were to send you into my office and give you one minute to find everything that is red. Sure enough, when you would come out you'd be ready to tell me about a red piece of fabric, the red lettering on a poster, the red cover of a book, a red marker, and a whole bunch of other red things that caught your eye.

But what would happen if you were to come out, with your mind so focused on remembering everything red, and I asked you to tell me everything in the room that was green.

You'd be stumped. You probably wouldn't have even seen many green things— and you would remember even fewer—because your focus had been so exclusively on things that were red.

That's just how our minds work. There is so much information that we are bombarded with every second of every day. The only way for our minds to operate is to delete anything that isn't relevant or important at that moment.

With your marriage it is the same.

You will only see what you are looking for.

Falling in love is the easy part. Staying in love takes work.

It requires a choice to overlook someone's weaknesses and focus on their greatness. When you focus more on their flaws and failures, it's only a matter of time before the love you started with erodes and is gone.

When you were courting, all you saw in this other person was what you liked. They were so amazing, and special, and the more you saw of them the more you liked them . . .

. . . And then you got married.

It might have happened slowly at first, but little by little things about them started to bug you. Maybe they were forgetful, or would say things that hurt you, or would leave socks on the floor, or would be late to events that were important to you.

If you have been married for more than six months, you have probably been let down enough times, and know enough things about your spouse that are reasons enough to call it quits and get divorced.

And if you choose to focus on those disappointments and shortcomings, they will not only make you and your spouse unhappy, they will also destroy anything positive about the relationship that was there.

I recently talked to a couple that after fifteen years of marriage were so focused on what they didn't like about each other that they couldn't see anything that they did like anymore. They couldn't even remember why they had gotten married in the first place.

Is that because those things weren't there anymore? No, their partners were still the same amazing, talented, beautiful people that they always were, they just could not see them that way any longer.

I call this having "*faulty filters.*"

It's as though you have a pair of glasses with lenses that are tinted deep red. When you wear them it's impossible to see other colors accurately.

With these faulty filters, even if your spouse is doing the right thing you will not be able to see it as right.

For example, if a wife is frustrated and believes that her husband is selfish, even if he does something nice—like wash the dishes, or bring her flowers—she may see it as him just trying to get something from her.

This is why you need to remove the faulty filters and begin to see your spouse as if *for the first time*, all over again.

I offered this couple what I call the "Gratitude Challenge." For thirty days they were to stop criticizing, nagging, or complaining about each other, and intentionally look for and acknowledge the specific things they respected and appreciated in their spouse.

It worked like magic.

At first they were resistant, but soon both the husband and wife began to praise each other. The husband took time to thank his wife for the incredible ways she cared for their children and for all her constant sacrifices to make their home comfortable. The wife, instead of nagging, began to acknowledge how hard her husband worked to provide for the family, and his amazing ability to fix things when they were broken.

Soon, they began to open up to each other, trust began to reemerge and they actually found themselves enjoying and looking forward to spending time together.

They learned that when you put your energy into focusing on what you like in the other person, you get more of that in return.

Does it mean there aren't things that still bug them about each other that they would like to change? No, it just means they consciously choose to overlook those and focus on the positive.

Focus on what you love and ignore what you don't. Fill yourself with gratitude for your spouse's greatness and all the good things that have come into your life because of their presence, and you will see why you are so lucky to be married to them.

THE PRACTICE:

Remember that each of these practices is not just a one-time gig. Marriage, like life, is an ongoing process of growth. To create an EPIC marriage, make it a daily commitment to practice seeing the best in your spouse. I encourage you to try the Gratitude Challenge and practice for thirty days withholding judgment and offering praise and encouragement.

Every day find time to cultivate an attitude of gratitude by identifying the best in your partner.

Start today by taking a few minutes to create a GRATITUDE LIST:

Make a list of ten specific things you love most about your spouse:

1)____

2)____

3)____

4)____

5)____

6)____

7)____

8)____

9)____

10)_______________________________________

Then choose one thing from this list and compliment them specifically on it today.

RESOURCES:

We can learn a lot from other people who have successful marriages. On our site we have collected many stories and lessons from those who have built EPIC marriages.

To read some of those stories and to share your own journey, breakthroughs, and experiences with us online, visit www.epic-marriage.com/stories

To access additional free content, bonuses, and other resources and ideas to help you focus on what you love about each other, visit www.epic-marriage.com

{ PRINCIPLE FIVE: }

IT'S NOT YOUR JOB TO FIX YOUR SPOUSE

> ***IT'S NOT YOUR JOB TO CHANGE OR FIX HER.*** *Your job is to love her as she is with no expectation of her ever changing. And if she does change, love what she becomes, whether it's what you wanted or not.*

There's an old joke that goes *"A woman gets married hoping her man will change and he doesn't. A man gets married hoping his woman won't change and she does."*

There's a lot of truth behind the humor.

The masculine energy is about stability, predictability, and order. The feminine energy is about growth, change, and expansion.

This can be beautiful and complimentary in a relationship, but honestly, most of the time it just causes frustration. The woman is constantly nagging the man hoping he'll change, and the man is constantly trying to control the woman.

I'm going to go out on a limb right now, and state the obvious: There are things you don't like about your spouse that you wish you could change.

Here's the reality: *You can't change anyone but yourself . . . and it's not your job to.*

No one wants to be fixed, and the attempt to do so will only cause frustration, pain, and bitterness.

When someone is the nagging wife or the controlling husband, it only creates resentment in both parties.

So listen up:

Women: *You are not his mother.*

Men: *She is not your property.*

Your happiness will be determined by how much you can appreciate what you have right now and not focusing on what you lack or are dissatisfied with. Let your spouse be independent and responsible for himself or herself. It's not your job to force them to fit your ideal.

This isn't to say that you can't help them grow and improve. As a team your goal IS to help each other be the best you can be. You should encourage each other and cheer each other on as you both grow and become better. And there should be space in a healthy relationship to offer and receive feedback from each other on how you can improve. If either spouse is acting in a way that is destructive to the relationship, you should be able to find a way to work together to fix those challenges before it becomes more of a problem.

You are both constantly evolving and growing, and the only way for your relationship to thrive is to support each other in a positive way.

Criticism and control will never get you the result you are looking for. When a wife speaks in a way that feels critical to her man, it is his "Anti-love Language," and it will cause him to feel unloved and unappreciated.

Here's a common example:

John comes home from work, stressed and preoccupied with work.

Jane, his wife, is exhausted after a day of caring for the many needs of their kids. Despite her weariness, she's prepared a nice dinner for the family.

John isn't very present during the meal, because his mind is still stuck on work and the things he needs to get done. Because of his mental absence, Jane feels disconnected, frustrated, and unappreciated.

After dinner, wanting to help somehow, John starts doing the dishes and empties the dishwasher, even though his mind is still distracted. Jane notices that he has put the measuring cups in by the glasses instead of where they should be.

Frustrated, she snaps, "Why did you put these here? This isn't where they go. How long have you lived here?"

Feeling hurt and offended, John walks off to go to his office, and they spend the rest of the night in an awkward silence.

A man's primary need in the relationship is to be **respected**.

He wants to be the **hero** that is there to provide, protect, and fix things for his woman. But when she expresses her dissatisfaction with his effort, he hears "*You are a failure. You can't make me happy. Nothing you do is good enough for me.*"

The natural response for a man in such situations is to either fight back and defend himself, or shut down. He may feel something like "*I'm just trying to help, and this is how I'm treated? Fine then, let her do it. Why should I help when I'm not appreciated?*" He then retreats to his man-cave to be alone, while the woman feels abandoned and unloved.

This may seem childish, but this is how scenarios like this play out. That's how the unconscious man and woman react.

So, as a wife, if you want change, instead of criticizing, focus on positive reinforcement and encouragement with your man. Let him know how much you appreciate him when he does something right. When he does the dishes, or helps you around the house to serve you, touch him affectionately and tell him "Thank you so much for doing that. It means a lot to me."

Make him feel like he is your **hero**, and he will keep doing those things.

If there is something he's doing that you want him to improve on, then suggest it in a way where he will still feel respected. Begin with appreciation and encouragement.

For example, what if Jane had responded something like this?

"I love when you help with the dishes." She lightly strokes the back of his neck. "I have been so stressed and exhausted, and I know you don't have to do it, so I really appreciate it,"

Then playfully she adds with a smile, "By the way, in the future, just in case you didn't know, the measuring cups go over here. If you ever don't know where something goes, just ask.

Thank you again, honey. You're my hero."

Women, most of you don't realize this, but we men are really easy to train. Reward us for what we do right and we'll want to do more. I thought about this when I was at Sea World and saw how they trained seals. Every time they do the right thing, they are given a fish so that they want to do it again. They are rewarded for what they do right with *positive reinforcement*

As I watched how those seals were trained, I thought, *I'm not much different than that.*

With your man, when he does something you like, let him know—praise him, touch him, reward him based on his love language and he will be eager to keep doing those things. But if you punish him, nag him, or try to "fix" him, it will just emasculate him, shut him down, and train him to avoid and distrust you. Criticism is like a poison poured on your garden which kills trust and intimacy.

You can't expect a positive result from a negative approach.

For you men, treat your woman like a gentle flower that will only fully blossom when she feels it is safe to do so.

The feminine energy is about change and expansion. Let her grow freely and you will be amazed at who she becomes. Shame her, or control her, and she will shut down and hide her blossoms from you.

The relationship will thrive most when both partners have the ability to fully be their unique selves.

You may not always agree with each other. You're not supposed to.

You may not do things the same way as your spouse. You're not supposed to.

It's the differences each spouse brings into the relationship that make it interesting, beautiful, and strong. Celebrate those differences and allow your partner to be who they are. Learn to appreciate what they bring to the relationship.

Focus on loving them the way they are now, and allow them to change as they will.

As they do change, focus on falling in love with the new person they have become.

THE PRACTICE:

When you realize that you have no power to change another person, you can see that all the change that you desire needs to come from within yourself.

In one of the events I conduct—a three-day breakthrough workshop called Live BIG—I show people how to create any change they wish to see in their lives by becoming "Conscious Creators." Your power to change your health, your relationships, or your wealth, comes from taking full responsibility and understanding your role as the creator of the results in your life.

Here's a process that will help you do some of the inner work on yourself when you feel someone else needs to change.

These are the four steps of Conscious Change:

STEP ONE: Acknowledgement

What is bothering you that you would like to change in your partner?

STEP TWO: Awareness

What is the need you think it would fill in you if they did change?

STEP THREE: Accountability

What has been your role, and what have you done to contribute to the problem?

STEP FOUR: Action

What can you do differently to get these needs fulfilled?

RESOURCES:

"The first step in Transforming your marriage is Transforming yourself."

If you are looking for ways to accelerate your personal growth and development, join me at my next Live BIG event.

Live BIG is a three-day transformational seminar designed to help you break through past limiting beliefs, understand who you truly are, discover your "soul purpose." In it you will consciously design the life you want to live, including your relationships, your health, and your money. One of my past attendees described it as "three years' worth of personal development packed into three days."

To find out more details and join us for the next Live BIG visit www.livebigseminar.com.

Learn how you can GET A FREE TICKET to attend Live BIG as well as help me on my mission to save marriages and become a Marriage Ambassador. For details visit www.epic-marriage.com/ambassador

{ PRINCIPLE SIX: }

TAKE FULL ACCOUNTABILITY FOR YOUR OWN EMOTIONS

> ***TAKE FULL ACCOUNTABILITY FOR YOUR OWN EMOTIONS.*** *It's not your wife's job to make you happy, and she* can't *make you sad. You are responsible for finding your own happiness, and through that your joy will spill over into your relationship and your love.*

"He makes me so mad." "She makes me so frustrated." "He makes me feel so bad about myself." "She makes me…(fill in the blank)."

I can't begin to say how many times I have seen and heard this pattern of blame show up in relationships, including my own. It's so easy in marriage to be triggered by the actions and words of our spouse and to have these emotions rise up.

But remember: *no one* can *make* you sad, or angry, or frustrated, or force you to feel anything else. These are *your* emotions. The moment you blame someone else for your unhappiness is the moment you lose your power to change it.

There is no power in playing the victim.

Your power comes from being accountable for your emotions and realizing that they are coming from within you.

Sure, your spouse may have done or said something that triggered you, but it was still your choice—even if it was an unconscious one—to react with the emotions that you did.

When you become a Conscious Creator and take ownership for the results of your life, including your own emotions, you *claim your power* and can take the steps to create something new. Then you can face and heal the problems you experience and be responsible for your own personal happiness.

As you do, you realize that it is *your job* to find happiness for yourself, and you have the power to be happy regardless of anything external in your life. Regardless of your finances, your kids, your spouse, your health, or any events, happiness is something you can choose to create right now.

In a codependent relationship you are constantly requiring and expecting your spouse to do things to fill you up. If you are waiting for your spouse to do certain things to make you happy and you are frustrated with the things they do to make you unhappy, you will be stuck in a powerless trap.

Get yourself out of that trap and take accountability for your own emotions.

You alone are responsible for your own happiness.

To choose happiness now means to focus on what you are grateful for. It means taking time to nurture yourself, and finding time to do what you love. Choosing happiness now means pursuing meaningful goals just because they are important to you.

When you choose to be responsible for your own happiness, you will find more joy in the relationships you have, but it will not come from a space of expectation or need. Instead you will discover that your happiness will flow over into ways that you can love and serve your spouse and family generously.

You cannot give from an empty cup. Most of our negative emotions come from being in a state of depletion. Fill yourself up to overflowing and you will have more than enough to share with your spouse, your kids, and those around you.

Think of when you are on an airplane and flight attendants are reviewing the safety instructions. There's a part when they show that in the event of a change in cabin pressure oxygen masks will come down. They instruct you to *first* put on your own oxygen mask and then to assist those around you.

It's not selfish to take care of yourself first. It's essential, and the only way you can fully offer your gifts and your love to those around you.

Find what makes you happy and pursue that. Encourage your spouse to do the same.

Your own happiness is the greatest gift you can bring into the relationship.

THE PRACTICE

As Conscious Creators we realize we are responsible for our own emotions. When we create happiness on our own, we bring more into the relationship. It's common, though, for people to lose themselves in marriage and to stop taking care of their own needs, which leaves them depleted and dependent. This shifts when you stop creating the expectation that it is your spouse's job to make you happy and you give yourself permission to *take care of yourself first.*

Create a **Self-Care List** of things that you can do to nurture your own happiness:

What did I like to do for fun before I got married?

What are some things I can do to nurture myself when I am feeling drained? (e.g. get a massage, take a hot bath, go for a run, spend some time in the mountains, go to a movie, read a good book....)

Brainstorm and list ten activities, interests, and hobbies that make you happy:

____

____

____

____

Schedule some personal time on your calendar right now to do some of these things this week. Make taking time to nurture yourself a priority every week, and encourage your spouse to do the same. Support each other in doing the things to fill yourselves up so you have plenty to give within the relationship.

RESOURCES:

For ideas on specific things you can do to nurture yourself, visit www.epic-marriage.com/resources.

In addition to finding more ideas for creating your Self-Care List you will also find training and access to other resources that will help you find more passion, fulfillment, and motivation in your life.

{ PRINCIPLE SEVEN: }

NEVER BLAME

NEVER BLAME YOUR WIFE IF YOU GET FRUSTRATED OR ANGRY AT HER; *it is only because it is triggering something inside of you. They are your emotions, and your responsibility. When you feel those feelings take time to get present and look within and understand what it is inside of you that is asking to be healed. You were attracted to this woman because she was the person best suited to trigger all of your childhood wounds in the most painful way so that you could heal them. When you heal yourself, you will no longer be triggered by her, and you will wonder why you ever were.*

Yes, I know. After reading the last chapter on taking accountability for your own emotions, this will sound redundant. But it is *that* important and cannot be said enough.

Taking full accountability for the results and experiences of our lives is the foundation of what it means to be a Conscious Creator and what is required to create an EPIC marriage and life.

When we point fingers and blame others for how we feel and what is happening in our lives and become victims, we give away our power and become power*less*.

Once again:

There is no power in being a victim.

All of your emotions, whether positive or negative, come from within you. They all are a reflection of deep, hidden subconscious beliefs that have been stored inside you since you were young.

There are thousands of limiting beliefs that we begin to adopt from the time we are born. You know those deep shadowy voices of discouragement inside your head that whisper *You're not good enough. You're not loveable. No matter how hard you try it will never be good enough. You can't trust others. You are ugly. You don't deserve to be happy…*

Any event, experience, or person that hurts you is just an external force that is triggering these deep inner beliefs that have been there for a long time.

When you look at your spouse, you probably notice that they seem to know all of the buttons to push to make you upset, and they often press them unconsciously.

One of my good friends, Tony Litster, who has spent years coaching people on relationships, once told me, "We are most attracted to that person who can trigger our childhood wounds in the most painful way so that we will do what it takes to heal."

What's great about knowing this is that when you realize that you are responsible for your emotions, then you realize that you have the power to change them.

So how do you do this? How do you heal from these inner wounds and these sabotaging beliefs?

I'm going to lay out this disclaimer: inner healing is a lifelong work. It won't happen overnight, but it can happen, regardless of how deep your pain might be.

It seems to me that we spend the first six years of our life taking on limiting beliefs that define who we are *not*, and the rest of our life trying to release them and remember who we truly are.

There are many different processes and modalities that assist with the healing of these inner wounds. Some of this work can be done on your own, and some will require a skilled coach or someone experienced in emotional healing that can help you see and work through the blocks you are experiencing.

THE 7 STEPS TO INNER HEALING

This is a powerful way as a Conscious Creator to deal with emotions as they are triggered in you.

The moment you notice a feeling of anger, frustration, sadness, etc., give yourself the time and space to work through those emotions before reacting. When we *react* to one of those negative emotions, we often will do or say things that damage the relationship further.

When emotions are *high,* reasoning is *low*. Be careful about the decisions you make and the way you react when you are in a high emotional state of sadness or anger.

When you are able to really work through your emotions in a healthy way, then you can *respond* in a manner that builds and nurtures intimacy rather than reacting in a way that destroys it.

Here's an example:

After a long day of work, Jen is anxious to unwind, have some dinner, and spend time with her husband, Mark. He tells her he will be home for dinner at six, but 6:00 comes and goes and he's nowhere to be seen. He doesn't text or call to tell her he's going to be late, and by 6:30 she is feeling angry, frustrated, and annoyed.

Fortunately, Jen is working on being a Conscious Creator and sees that her emotions aren't about Mark at all. She knows that if she is still feeling this way when he gets home it would be easy for her to yell or say something that would ruin the rest of their night, so she decides to take a break and work through her emotions.

Step 1) **Become aware of the emotion and identify it**. What exactly are you feeling and what is that emotion telling you?

(Underneath the anger and frustration, Jen identified the feelings of disappointment and not being appreciated.)

Step 2) **Identify the trigger**. What exactly happened or was said that made you feel this way?

(For Jen, it was Mark not coming home when she expected him to, and the bad thoughts of all things he might have been doing instead of spending time with her.)

Step 3) **Find the root belief**. What would you have to believe to feel this way?

(Jen saw that beneath the emotion was the belief that she wasn't valued, that she wasn't a priority, and that she wasn't loveable.)

Step 4) **Where did the belief come from**? When did this *really* begin? Most of our current emotions come from beliefs that we adopted as a child. When did you first start to believe this?

(Jen realized that when she was a child, she really wanted love and attention from her dad, but her dad never seemed to be available because he seemed to always be working. As a little girl, she began to believe that she wasn't worth it, because her dad was too busy to spend time with her.)

Step 5) **What do I want?** If you see that these beliefs are causing pain and frustration, what are the emotions and results you really want to have?

(Jen decided what she really wanted was to feel love and peace. She wanted to have a great evening with Mark and for him to feel how much she loved him.)

Step 6) **Find the antidote.** If these limiting beliefs are the toxins that are poisoning you, what are the healing and empowering beliefs that would create the emotion and result you want?

(Jen saw that she could choose to believe she is important, that she is unconditionally loveable, and that she is always in control of her life. And that while Mark isn't perfect, he is doing the best he can.)

STEP 7) **What do I do?** What are the next steps you can take that will help you create the reality that you want?

(Jen realized that in order to create the loving connection and enjoyable, peaceful evening with Mark she needed to express love to him when he got home and look for meaningful ways to connect with him.)

When Mark finally came in the door at 6:45, Jen was back to a space of peace and love, and rather than barking at him for being late, she ran up to give him a hug and welcome him home. He apologized for not being on time because traffic was terrible and his cell phone was dead, so he couldn't call her and let her know.

They ended up having a fantastic dinner, enjoying some time together that evening, and making love. When they finally fell asleep in each other's arms, both were very happy and content.

(Yes, this is how I think all good stories should end.)

People raise their eyebrows at first when I say this, but I don't believe there are bad emotions. There are many emotions that we don't like, but that doesn't make them bad. Being angry, or sad, or frustrated isn't wrong, it is simply a signal that says that something inside of us is off and needs to be changed.

Emotional responsibility doesn't mean that you should stuff or repress your anger or frustration. Burying emotions may cause additional problems, whether volatile eruptions, or even physical and health challenges. I'm just encouraging you to deal with your emotions in a healthy way for you and the relationship.

Emotional responsibility means that we recognize that our emotions belong to us and we are fully accountable for them, understanding that there are healthy and unhealthy ways to deal with them.

Sometimes if you are really angry, finding a place to yell and scream and hit a pillow can be the cathartic release you need to get back to where you can think clearly. Sometimes exercise can be a tool to rebalance. At other times meditation or a hot bath or a walk in nature may help you release. Find what works for you, and when you are triggered, rather than reacting from the emotion, create the space you need in order to think clearly and work through your feelings.

If you blame your spouse and release your anger on them, however, it violates the intimacy and trust in the relationship and is just like pouring poison on your garden. Negative actions and negative works cannot produce a positive result.

If your spouse is doing or saying something that continues to trigger you or hurt your marriage, you should have the ability in your relationship to communicate openly about it. Hopefully there is a level of respect and love where you can work through the issues together and heal the emotion and change the behaviors that are triggering you.

THE PRACTICE:

One of the most important skills to have in life is learning to be a Conscious Creator through **self-awareness**. When you can notice the emotions you are experiencing and realize they are coming from inside of you, then you can stop looking outside for the solutions, and do the work of finding the real root of the emotions. We call these "triggers."

Most of the time, when we are being triggered by someone else, it is because they have touched a raw nerve inside of us connected to limiting beliefs that we have adopted at some previous point in our life. When we see that it is not them, but the beliefs from our past that are the real problems, then we can start healing in a meaningful way.

Find the Triggers

Think of a recent time your spouse did something and you felt angry, frustrated or sad.

1: What exactly happened? What did they say or do?

2: How did it make you feel?

3: What did you feel it meant about you?
(I'm not lovable, I'm not good enough. I can't get my needs met. No matter how hard I try it's never enough…)

4: When is the earliest time you remember feeling that way? *(What is the event from your childhood or your past that is being triggered?)*

5: What else could you choose to believe that would help you feel the way you want?

6. What specific things can you do to help create the reality you want?

RESOURCES:

At my events and through the various coaching I offer, we do many exercises to help you begin your deep healing work, starting you on the path to becoming a more powerful and aware Conscious Creator.

One of my seminars that I lead several times a year is a three-day breakthrough event called Live BIG. During that event we dive deep into exploring who you really are, and identifying the inner limiting beliefs that hold you back from experiencing your full brilliance and what you want in life. Then we learn some practical tools and processes to reprogram your subconscious to support you in creating new results in your life. We also work on defining your "soul purpose" in life and the goals that will move you forward.

The Live BIG Breakthrough Seminar is a unique experience that will allow you to explore what is really possible in your life and to overcome the blocks that have held you back in the past. I love seminars because they create an accelerated-learning environment where you can do the deep, personal inner work that you couldn't do alone.

If you feel like you need additional support in healing, overcoming your limiting beliefs and discovering who you are and what is possible in your life, consider coming to Live BIG.

To find out when the next one is visit www.LiveBigSeminar.com. Use the promo code "BOOKSPECIAL" to receive a 50% discount off the normal price. Or discover how you can attend for free by becoming a Marriage Ambassador at www.epic-marriage.com/ambassador

Coming as a couple will be one of the best things you ever do for your marriage.

You can also learn more about our coaching programs and events by visiting www.epic-marriage.com/mentoring

{ PRINCIPLE EIGHT: }

ALLOW YOUR WOMAN TO JUST BE

ALLOW YOUR WOMAN TO JUST BE. *When she's sad or upset, it's not your job to fix it, it's your job to hold her and let her know it's okay. Let her know that you hear her, that she's important, and that you are that pillar on which she can always lean. The feminine spirit is about change and emotion and, like a storm, her emotions will roll in and out. As you remain strong and nonjudgmental, she will trust you and open her soul to you.* ***Don't run away when she's upset****. Stand present and strong and let her know you aren't going anywhere. Listen to what she is really saying behind the words and emotion.*

There is an epic failure in most marriages to truly understand the needs of our partners.

Men and women have such different core needs, it's like they speak different languages.

It's only by learning to truly listen and understand what the other is saying that we achieve true, lasting intimacy.

Women, at their core, yearn to be *loved* and *cherished*. They want to feel safe and protected. They desire to be really understood, appreciated, and validated.

They are primarily emotional thinkers and are continually growing and changing, and they work through their challenges and stress best when they can talk about them.

Men, on the other hand, want to be *respected*. They want to be the *hero* who saves the day and has their lady praising how great they are. They want to create stability, balance, and order and when something is wrong they want to "fix it."

Men are primarily logical and linear. When they see a problem, their masculine drive kicks in and the first thing they try to figure out is the fastest way to solve it. When a man is experiencing a personal challenge or stress, he will typically withdraw and go into his man-cave to think about it.

In a conscious marriage, this is a beautiful and synergistic match. It is a perfect balance that allows both parties to contribute something meaningful and for this incredible polarity of attraction to draw them closer together.

Unfortunately, most marriages are *not* conscious and these two different natures are a recipe for friction, conflict, and marital chaos.

Imagine this scenario that is played out in a million ways, a million times every day:

Woman is frustrated and emotional.

Man wants to help.

Woman begins to express her frustration.

Man offers solution to fix it.

Woman gets more upset because she doesn't feel heard or validated.

Man feels like he is not being respected, can't be the hero, and withdraws.

Woman feels like she can't trust her man and emotionally disconnects.

This disharmony then creeps into many other issues in the relationship, such as sex, money, and communication.

A woman's emotion is always changing, like the weather. Some days it is sunny and bright, other days it is dark and stormy—and sometimes the weather can change from moment to moment. Much of the time, when she's upset, she doesn't know what she wants or needs to fix it.

The man wants his woman to be sunny and happy all the time, because to him that is a sign that he is doing his job well. When she's not happy, he feels like something is wrong and needs to change it, and when he can't chase the storm clouds away he feels like a failure.

What the man fails to realize is that when his woman is expressing an emotion, she needs to feel it and express it. Many times she just wants to be understood, and not have it fixed. It is one of her ways to experience connection. For her, what she is really wanting is a man who can stand in the face of the storm and not run away. She needs a space where it is safe for her to verbalize what she is feeling without being judged or proven wrong, whether it is rational or not. When she has that space, the emotion will pass like a storm cloud that quickly moves out, leaving this beautiful, fresh, clean feeling. When that space is not there, she will bottle up the emotions and the storm will continue to build within her until it can no longer be contained.

Oftentimes, when she comes to her man to express a problem or feeling, she is not looking for a solution at all… and sometimes she is.

This is where advanced communication skills come in—the type that sound obvious except in the moment.

Here are some great things you can do to create that space for authentic and intimate communication:

WOMEN: Don't expect your man to be a mind reader. Even after he's lived with you for years and years, he still won't intuitively know what you need. Know that his primary instinct when you express frustration is going to be to take it personally and try to fix it. Before you talk to him, get clear on what you really want and let him know, then find a time to talk that works for both of you.

If you just need him to talk and for him to *listen*, try something like this: "Honey, I'm wondering if we could talk. I'm feeling really frustrated and overwhelmed right now, and it would mean a lot to me if you would just be willing to listen. I'm not needing you to fix anything, I just need to feel understood."

And if you *do* need him to offer solutions (which he loves), say something like this: "Honey, I'm wondering if you have a few minutes to talk. I am feeling frustrated about this problem and would love to get your input on what I should do."

And if you want him to actually do something: "Honey, do you have a few minutes to talk? I have this problem I need some help with, and I know you are really good with this type of thing."

The more you can make him feel successful and respected, the more eager he will be to do what you want. Remember he *wants* to feel like a hero to you. Make it easy for him to do so.

MEN: Know that your woman will have emotions, and that's a good thing. You don't really want it to be sunny all the time. I mean, that would be so boring, right?

The more you can stand strong in your masculinity and allow her to go through her emotions without feeling judged or wrong for them, the more she will trust you and open up to you. The more she's able to open up to you, the less she will bottle up those emotions, and so the storms will pass faster.

But do not expect her to always tell you what she wants, and do not think you have to be a mind reader.

When she comes to you with a frustration, simply ask her, "I want to make sure I can support you and understand you best, so tell me, do you want me to help you find a solution or just listen?"

She may not know, in which case just listen and validate her, and then afterwards if she still needs your opinion, you can ask her if she wants it.

Your job is to really understand her and why she is feeling the way she is. Ask questions, get her talking as much as possible, and just actively listen. Let her know that you understand by saying things like:

"Wow, that must be really hard."

"Tell me more…"

"I'm sorry you had to experience that."

"So you're saying that…"

"Really? I am so sorry that you felt that way."

"Oh, that would make me so mad too. I totally get it."

"I can understand how you would feel that."

Etc…

Guys, I hope you realize how valuable these little phrases are! These are the things that create emotional intimacy and trust for a woman, and that is what leads to physical intimacy, so this is a skill worth mastering. Sometimes, when I teach guys that the way to have more sex with their wife is to learn to be a better listener, they look at me doubtfully, but then they try it and tell me that they can't believe they didn't figure this out earlier. I have no idea why I didn't learn earlier either. I think this alone would have made a huge difference in my marriage.

Be fully present with her as she talks. Be sincere. Look into her eyes, nod your head in understanding, and hold her hand so she feels connected.

Realize the real problem you are trying to fix *isn't* the problem she is talking about. The real issue is making her feel validated and appreciated. When you realize the way to "fix" the problem and be the hero for her is just by listening and understanding her, you will become very good at this.

And don't forget the value of a good strong hug, where you can just hold her and let her know it's okay. She needs to feel the firm strength you carry so she can relax into her femininity.

On the flipside, when men are dealing with stress or frustration, rather than talking about it, they often prefer to retreat to their man-cave and have some time alone.

Men, if you are dealing with a challenge and you need space, just let her know.

Say, "Hey, I'm really frustrated about something right now, and I just need some space to think. I'm going to take some time for myself right now, so that when I come back I can be more present for you, okay?"

Women, if your man is struggling with something, there may be times when he needs to talk to you about it, and other times, he'll just want to work through it himself.

You can help your man by saying, "I can tell something is bothering you right now. Would you like to talk about it, or would you prefer some time alone?"

These are simple, yet invaluable skills of communication in relationships.

THE PRACTICE:

Understanding the core needs of men versus women is critical for an EPIC marriage. Every person and every relationship is different though, and there is no universal box that every marriage can fit in.

Despite the fact that we live with someone of the opposite sex for years and years, there's still so much that we don't understand about who they are and what their needs are. This is why communication and education is so vital.

It takes time and effort to really understand your partner and their needs. And the moment you think you have it figured out, it will probably change.

Take time to define the ways you want your spouse to show up for you when you are in your emotional storms. What can they do and say to make you feel loved and validated? Then commit to communicate those needs to your spouse in a clear, positive way.

Here are some open-ended statements that will help you better communicate your needs and desires to your spouse:

When I feel upset or angry what I want you to do is . . .

When I am feeling overwhelmed and stressed the things you can do for me are . . .

When I am feeling depressed and sad the things you can do to help are . . .

RESOURCES:

We have created a series of free audios to train you on the skills of successful relationships, including communication. To access my *free* audio training on the power of effective communication as a couple and other bonus audios, please visit www.epic-marriage.com/resources

{ PRINCIPLE NINE: }

BE SILLY

> ***BE SILLY.*** *Don't take yourself so damn seriously. Laugh. And make her laugh. Laughter makes everything else easier.*

When I was courting my wife, I was so much fun. I always had creative ideas for dates. I was spontaneous and clever, and nothing made me happier than hearing her laugh.

Years into my marriage, I remember looking at myself and asking, "How on earth did I get to be so boring?"

The stress of work, bills, and raising a family had caused me make the terrible mistake of becoming what I thought a grown-up was supposed to be: *boring*. I had lost touch with the spontaneous, witty, playful, and curious side of my personality, which was a critical part of what had made me and my marriage feel alive.

Fun and laughter are some of the most important ingredients in a thriving relationship. When things get routine, or when there is stress in the marriage, lightheartedness quickly vanishes.

Want to ease a tense situation? Then make the other person laugh. No one can stay mad when they are laughing.

Want to release stress? Laugh.

Want to connect more deeply with your spouse? Find moments to laugh together.

They even say laughter will help you live longer, and even if that weren't true, at least it helps make the time you are alive more worth living.

For many people, laughter is one of the most important ways that they feel loved and connected . . . so lighten up. Don't take yourself so seriously. Smile and enjoy this moment.

Find and celebrate the humor in everyday life.

THE PRACTICE:

It's funny to think that you might need to practice being silly, but I know it helps me. More than anything, think of this as your permission to embrace and nurture your inner child, that healthy, creative, fun and inspirational part of who you are.

When you feed that fun, spontaneous, and enjoyable part of your marriage it will help create greater intimacy in all areas. Think of some crazy date ideas that you can enjoy as a couple.

Here are some ideas and a chance to create your own:

- Take some crazy photos together, seeing who can make the silliest faces
- Watch an old comedy from the 80's (preferably something with Bill Murray)
- Spend an evening on the town dressed up in some crazy costume that represents your alter ego
- Visit a local art gallery and playfully critique the art, coming up with wacky explanations for what it means
- Get some Play-Doh or clay and play "Sculptionary," where you give each other questions, (i.e. what's your favorite sport?), sculpt the answer, then guess what your spouse made.

- Thrift store scavenger hunt: Make a list of random things and go to local thrift stores or pawn shops and see how many you can find

- Go to a nickel-cade or Chuck E. Cheese and have a skee-ball competition

- Pick a theme for the night and dress up in outfits, play games and cook a meal based on the theme (cowboy, Hawaiian, retro, etc.)

- Karaoke night out (wearing costumes is always a bonus)

- Go to a comedy club and sit in the front row

- Go to an amusement park, fair, or festival that you've never been to before

- Bad art night: Get a bunch of art and craft supplies and go crazy

- Get some old 70's clothes from the thrift shop and go roller-skating

- Blindfolded bumper-bowling competition

- Make your own kites and fly them in a park

Now it's your turn. What are the craziest and most fun ideas you can think of?

RESOURCES:

For a full list with more than sixty date ideas from the Romantic to the Ridiculous, and other great ways to spice up your love life visit: www.epic-marriage.com/resources

{ PRINCIPLE TEN: }

FILL HER SOUL EVERY DAY

> ***FILL HER SOUL EVERY DAY.*** *Learn her love languages and the specific ways that she feels important and validated and cherished. Ask her to create a list of ten things that make her feel loved. Memorize those things and make it a priority every day to make her feel like a queen.*

For each of us, there are specific things that make us feel loved, and natural ways in which we express our love.

Do you really know your spouse's "love recipe"? What makes them feel *truly loved*?

I remember being shocked after fifteen years of marriage when I realized that I had no idea.

And so, even though I deeply loved this woman, my attempts to show it were scattered and often missed the mark. I would give her a hug, snuggle with her, and say "I love you" nearly every day, because physical touch and words of affirmation were my love languages, but they weren't hers, and so it meant very little in filling up her love tank. And then there were so many times during our marriage that I simply got busy, or distracted, or lazy, and I stopped trying to make her feel loved on a daily basis.

Like all of us, she needed to feel that love consistently in a way that made her know she was validated, cherished, and appreciated. That could only come through me figuring out her "love recipe."

Imagine the love in your marriage is like this tender plant you are growing in your garden. It's obviously a top priority to water and take care of it every day, so why is it that you neglect it so often?

Why is it we don't make a more focused effort every day to ensure our spouse really feels loved?

Why is it so easy for us to get lazy in love?

I believe that

love is always either growing or dying, and it only grows when we nurture and invest in it.

So, have you really learned your spouse's "love recipe"?

What are the specific things that make her feel cherished and adored? What are the things that make him feel like he's on top of the world?

Understanding how your spouse really feels loved and validated is one of the most important things you will ever learn.

Gary Chapman, in his best-selling book, *The Five Love Languages*, identifies the love languages as Physical Touch, Words of Affirmation, Acts of Service, Quality time, and Receiving Gifts.

The challenge is that most people *give* love based on their own love language and not that of their spouse's. And so even if they are trying to say *I love you*, their spouse isn't able to hear it.

When you know the language they receive love in, it makes it easier for you to win.

We all receive love at some level through each of these channels. But we all have a *primary* and *secondary* love language which are the ways we most naturally experience love. Understanding these will allow you to know how to both speak and receive love with your spouse.

Here are some examples of how to "speak love" through these different dialects:

PHYSICAL TOUCH: Cuddling up while watching a movie, lightly rubbing her arm, holding hands in public, planting a spontaneous kiss when you walk past, giving him a big hug when he walks in the door, rubbing the back of her neck while driving in the car, scratching his back during church, giving her a relaxing or sensual massage after a long day, long firm hugs anytime, or dancing in the kitchen just for the heck of it.... and, of course, sex.

WORDS OF AFFIRMATION: Random notes hidden in his jacket pocket to be discovered in the middle of the day, genuine and sincere compliments, speaking the words "*I love you*" often, sticky notes on the mirror that remind her how beautiful she is, saying "Thank you, that means a lot to me when you . . .", bragging about how proud you are of him to others when he's within earshot, posts on Facebook about how lucky you are to have a wife like her.

ACTS OF SERVICE: Working together on a project that is important to him, doing the dishes for her and cleaning the kitchen at the end of a long day, taking care of that chore they really don't want to do, secretly cleaning his car, breakfast in bed on Saturday morning, asking what you can help her cross things off her to-do list, taking care of him when he's sick, and anything that shows you are thinking ahead and doing something to make her life easier.

QUALITY TIME: Enjoying dinner out together, sitting down at the end of the day to share what is going on, scheduling time to Skype while you are away from each other, inviting friends over for a game night, taking time out of a busy day to just check in and let her know you are thinking about her, walking around the neighborhood holding hands, working together on fun hobbies or projects, watching your favorite show and laughing together, finding a service project you can team up on, pillow talk at the end of the day and anything else that is one-on-one that shows them that your spouse is a priority to you.

RECEIVING GIFTS: Bringing flowers home from work, a memorable gift when you travel, thoughtful surprises that show you have been thinking about them, a delicious treat you buy just for him, a fun new outfit, things for the home to celebrate the season, jewelry or a watch, a gift card, a treasure hunt with clues around the house for him to find a surprise gift, and things that show you know what she likes.

Remember, we each have primary and secondary love languages, and each of us receives love in some degree through *all* of these.

The important thing is to consciously express love often, and to do it in a way that means love to your spouse.

I've often seen it in my life and in others' where we are attempting to express love to our spouse through *our* love language, but it means very little because it's not *theirs*.

For example, if a man tries to show love by giving his wife jewelry, but neglects her love languages of quality time and acts of service, the wife still won't feel loved and cherished because of the gift.

If a man's primary love language is physical touch and words of affirmation, and his wife expresses her love by cleaning the house and talking to him, he will not feel fulfilled and loved.

When you do figure out your spouse's love language, then make it a conscious effort to show her that kind of love every day.

Speaking your spouse's love language is like watering this plant in the garden. It's critical you water it often, but *don't overwater it.* Sometimes, when the plant is withering, in fear we try to overdo it and end up drowning it. In the same way, your exuberance can make your spouse feel smothered. Trust your intuition and find the right amount of love to give.

THE PRACTICE:

Identify your and your spouse's primary love language.

I recommend using the simple online test created by Gary Chapman, author of *The Five Love Languages*, which can be found at www.5lovelanguages.com.

Ask your spouse to make a list of ten specific things that make them feel loved.

1)____

2)____

3)____

4)____

5)____

6)____

7)____

8)____

9)____

10)_______________________________________

Pick one thing from this list to express love to your spouse today (and then every day after that).

RESOURCES:

For a link to Gary Chapman's best-selling book and more recommended reads and other resources to help you understand how to better communicate love in your relationship, visit www.epic-marriage.com/resources

{ PRINCIPLE ELEVEN: }

BE PRESENT

> ***BE PRESENT.*** *Give her, not only your time, but your focus, your attention and your soul. Do whatever it takes to clear your head so that when you are with her you are **fully*** with her. *Treat her as you would your most valuable client. She is.*

All of our power is found in the present moment. Too often though, we are so lost in the past, or worried about the future that we are anywhere but right here.

We come home from the day but our thoughts are still in the past.

As we enter our houses, our minds are still stuck on the conversations or the problems at work and we keep thinking about disappointments and drama from days or months ago. If we had a conflict with someone, it keeps rewinding and replaying in our head like a broken record.

We also get consumed with the stresses of tomorrow.

Our minds are processing all the things on our to-do list, to finish the projects that we have. We are worried about how to pay our bills or tackle other problems. Or we have an idea that we've gotten really excited about.

And then we are bombarded with a thousand distractions in our environment: the noise on the radio, the shows on TV, the magazines, the mail, the chores around the house, Facebook, friends, church—and all the other clutter and things that fill our lives.

Being a parent compounds this even more, because rather than just being worried about your own life, you're worried about your kids' lives as well.

Each of these things in your mind is called an *open loop*. Your mind craves completion and order just as it does when you start a story and want to know how it ends. With these unfinished stories cluttering your brain, it becomes nearly impossible to fully connect with your spouse, and when you are with her but not present, it makes it seem as though she's miles away and unimportant to you.

You know how frustrating this feels, don't you? Recall when you've had a conversation with someone and you can tell they are only half there. They may nod every once in a while, but you can tell their mind is on something else.

And you also know how it feels to be that person who is not fully present in the conversation.

Guys, we're notorious for this, and our women hate it. They want to feel cherished and important—like they are the most important thing in our lives. When we fail to be truly present with them, it makes them feel worthless.

Men typically tend to focus only on one thing at a time. Being able to create a separation from work and home is hard. We put so much of ourselves into our work that when we come home it's like we need a switch for our brains that will put us into *Husband* and *Father* mode.

For women, your challenge is that you have so many things going on in your brain at all times that being able to set them all aside to be fully present and engaged with your husband is a challenge. When your mind is consumed with taking care of the kids, dealing with your work, managing your house, worrying about your finances, and everything else, how much is left to give to your spouse?

What helps is when you have an awareness and can communicate openly, and figure out a strategy that helps you clear your mind.

For the men, to clear your mind so you can be more present, maybe that means a little bit of quiet transition time after they get home to help you switch roles.

For the women, it could mean asking your spouse to listen and talk to you at the end of the day, (without trying to fix anything for you) while you sort out and share everything that's on your mind.

For both, it means shutting off your phone, turning off the TV, and being able to focus on creating a meaningful connection free of distractions.

And it means having a clear intention to be *fully present* with your spouse whenever you are with them.

Always remember, your spouse is the most important person in your life. Make them feel that way.

All of our power is found in the present moment.

THE PRACTICE:

Here is a powerful communication exercise to help you practice connecting and staying present.

This may feel unnatural and forced at first, but as you become more adept in knowing how to communicate and listen, it will become easier.

Remember guys, even though you have an urge to fix everything when you listen to her problems, resist, because the way to really *fix things is by simply seeking to understand and validate her. This is how you become the hero. This is how to make her open up and be intimate with you.*

As a couple:

Set aside time together where you can be in a place without distractions.

Begin with the wife speaking and the husband listening.

Set a timer and give your wife five or ten minutes to dump whatever is on her mind. During that time, resist the urge to defend, correct, fix her problems, offer solutions, or space out. Your goal is simply to be present and to encourage her to share as much as possible.

After the time is up, switch roles.

Use phrases like this to encourage sharing and to validate their feelings.

"Wow, that must be hard."

"How did you handle that?"

"How did that make you feel?"

"I can't believe it."

"That's pretty amazing."

"You must be really struggling with that."

"That must be challenging."

"So, just to make sure I'm following you . . ."

"So you're saying . . . "

"You're feeling like . . . "

"What I'm hearing you say is…"

RESOURCES:

Communication is one of the core foundations for a successful relationship and yet it's a neglected subject. I've created powerful and fun audio training on how to communicate more effectively with the opposite sex. To download this free resource, visit www.epic-love.com/resources

{ PRINCIPLE TWELVE: }

BE WILLING TO TAKE HER SEXUALLY

> ***BE WILLING TO TAKE HER SEXUALLY,*** *to carry her away in the power of your masculine presence, to consume her and devour her with your strength, and to penetrate her to the deepest levels of her soul. Let her melt into her feminine softness as she knows she can trust you fully.*

Warning: I'm going to talk very openly and unapologetically about sex. I'm going to say all the things your parents should've said to you, but didn't, probably because it was a taboo subject, they were embarrassed, or they didn't understand it themselves.

Sexual intimacy is a core foundation of a healthy marriage.

Sex can and should be one of the most fulfilling, fun, and connecting experiences in a marriage. It is a core drive and desire that draws men and women together and bonds them in a powerful way.

Yet, sex is also one of the primary areas that couples struggle in their relationship, and one of the main sources of unhappiness and dysfunction.

One of the main reasons is because of how few people talk openly about it. Very few couples openly discuss their desires and needs, and very few men or women know how to be great lovers in and out of the bedroom. There is hardly any really good sex education out there, and much of what is taught is wrong.

This needs to change.

Growing up in a Christian culture often we adopt the wrong ideas about sex. We hear "Sex is bad," "Sex is dirty," "Don't talk about sex," but at the same time we know that God has ordained sex as a sacred way for us to connect at the most intimate level with our spouse, and to experience the most Godlike experience we have as humans, being able to create life with someone else.

Good, loving, and passionate sex is one of the core elements for a happy, enduring EPIC marriage, one with a deep Emotional Physical and Intellectual Connection. No marriage can be healthy or sustained without it.

Sex is an anchor that connects the soul of the man and the women in the most intimate and personal way. It creates a sacred bond and a union with your spouse that can only come through this physical connection. The more connected and consistent sexual intimacy you have, the greater your union, bond, and love becomes.

Research has shown that sex has many other health benefits as well:

- It helps relieve stress and decrease anxiety by releasing a chemical in our brains called dopamine and oxytocin, which are feel-good hormones.
- It strengthens your immune system and can lower your blood pressure.
- It improves sleep and relaxation.
- It is a great form of exercise and can burn 85-250 calories. (If you have sex for fifteen minutes at least three times a week you may burn over 7,500 calories in a year which is equivalent to jogging seventy-five miles!)
- It reduces the chance of heart disease and lowers high blood pressure.
- It keeps you healthier. (Immunoglobin A, an antigen that fights the flu increases when the frequency of sex increases).
- It makes you look and feel younger.
- It enhances your self-esteem.

- It bonds a couple and increases a sense of trust and connection.

- It increases mental clarity and creativity.

- Studies have shown that good, frequent sex—three or more times a week—can even increase your life expectancy by 3-8 years. (You do want to live longer and healthier, don't you?)

- PLUS, it just feels really, really amazing.

Most people want good, healthy, passionate and loving sex, so why is it that so many couples struggle with this?

Men and women seem to be wired differently around sex.

Women require emotional connection and intimacy first, before they are ready to open fully and engage physically in sex.

On the other hand, the physical intimacy of sex is the bridge to open men's emotions.

In order for sex and intimacy to really work in a relationship, it requires open communication and a desire to meet the other's needs.

Here's what every couple should know about sex:

Contrary to what many men believe, nearly all women desire sex, but even more than that, they crave true *intimacy*.

They want passionate, deeply connected intimacy in all forms—physical, emotional, intellectual and spiritual. And they want you as their man to be able to step up in a powerful and masculine way to make them feel sexy and cherished, so they can trust you and surrender themselves completely to you.

But most men have *no clue* how to be good lovers and how to unlock that passionate, sensual, sexy goddess-energy of their wife.

The sexual experience for every woman is a little different, though there are many core similarities. And even with your woman, it won't be the same every time. She will need variety and change. There will probably never come a time where you have it all figured out. It's that ability to go with the flow, and be spontaneous and to create new experiences together that makes sex such a magical part of your relationship.

Understand that every relationship is different and almost always partners in the marriage will have different drives and needs with sex. The important thing is to communicate openly as a team to find a way to make sure each of you feels loved and respected in this area.

This is **THE ADVICE I WISH I WOULD'VE HAD ABOUT SEX:**

FOR THE MEN:

In order for a woman to *open up sexually* you need to create a space of *trust,* of *safety,* a place where she feels *loved* and *desired.* If she doesn't feel these things, it's not likely that she'll want to have sex with you.

Her body is like a door to the deepest parts of her soul, and the only way she will want you to enter in is if she feels she can trust you.

As a conscious lover this is your job. Here's how:

1) **Women need to feel connected emotionally first** before they are ready to connect physically. For a woman, her primary need is to feel cherished and validated. The more you can take time to listen to her and connect with her, with the intent to fill that need, without trying to fix anything, the more she will open up to you.

2) **Help her clear her mind**. The mind of a woman is scattered between so many things—her kids, the house, her work, and all of the projects and responsibilities of life. In order for her to be present and open sexually, she needs to be able to clear her mind. To help her gather her thoughts, take time to talk to her, listen to her, help her clean the house or get her projects done, and create an environment with minimal distractions where she can relax. This will help her to be able to let go and focus on you.

3) **Real foreplay starts outside the bedroom**. It may take a long time for a woman to warm up and be ready for sex. Men are like microwaves with a switch that's easy to turn on. Women are like an oven and take a lot more time to warm up. It's all the little things that happen throughout the day that make her ready and desiring to have sex with you.

Your goal is to make her feel cherished and let her know that you find her attractive.

Here are some ideas to build her desire for you: Leave a surprise note for her that she'll find. Send her a spontaneous text to let her know you're thinking of her. Call and check in to let her know you love her. Flirt with her. Help her with things that are important to her. Be a great listener. Tell her how sexy she is to you. Give her a specific compliment that makes her feel attractive to you (i.e. "Wow, you look fantastic! That dress is so hot on you." "Have I told you lately how amazing I think your eyes are?" "Mmm. You smell delicious.")

4) Focus on non-sexual touch first. This is the key to make her want you sexually. It's the warmth of a hug or an arm around her shoulder, the gentle touch on the back of her neck, the light stroke of your fingers on her arm, the warmth of your hand resting on her leg that makes the rest of her body want to be touched. One of the secrets of touch is to start and stop. For instance, begin rubbing her back, and then stop and pull your hand away while staying present with her. When you pull away, it makes her want more. It's the combination between the soft gentle caress and the strong firm touch that makes it exciting for her. When you touch her in safe non-sexual areas of her body, it begins to make her want your touch on the rest of her body.

5) She needs to feel like **you don't care if you have sex or not**. The thing that will draw her in and ready to open up is if she feels totally safe is when she knows that you are not just trying to get something from her. If you can give this love to her, create a space for her to relax, and not be attached to whether sex happens or not, it makes you incredibly

attractive and allows her to relax into her feminine nature. Women are intuitive beings, so you really need to be okay with giving and loving her without any attachment to whether or not it will lead to sex.

6) **Don't worry about rejection, just look for one "yes" at a time**. If you jump straight to asking for sex without doing everything else, she will probably not be interested, so don't be surprised when she says no.

Think of it this way. She is biologically programmed to say no. In the days before birth control, a woman could get pregnant every time she had sex, so she had to say no often. When she said yes, it needed to be with a man that demonstrated patience so that he would be a good mate in taking care of the kids.

A "no" doesn't mean she doesn't love you, or that she's not interested, it just means you need to start doing the other little things to help her feel safe and cherished and connected emotionally so she's ready. Start with filling up her love tank in meaningful ways and with a light touch to make her know you really care. She will give you signs that say she's enjoying it. From there you can move to hugging. And then the kiss, and then making out, and then to carrying her to the bedroom and making passionate love to her. One step at a time. You can't skip straight to home plate without going to the other bases first.

7) **Go slower than you think you should**. When you go slow, versus rushing or forcing it, it creates a feeling of safety and anticipation for the woman.

Staying connected throughout the day, and intentionally building the sense of intimacy through communication and non-sexual touch, will help her to warm up and be excited to have sex with you.

When you are in the bedroom, rather than going straight for intercourse, spend a lot of time on foreplay, touching her, massaging her, kissing her, and making her feel sexy and desired. When you do this right you will awaken in her sexual desire she may not even know she had. Be a patient lover, and watch her blossom in the bedroom.

Being a good lover also means to be patient *after* intercourse. After they release, men are typically ready to move on, but women want time to process and enjoy the connection. Stay present with her, hold her, and tell her that you love her.

8) Nothing is sexier than confidence. Women are drawn to confident men. Men who know who they are, who show up *authentically* and unapologetically in life, and exude confidence in how they talk, walk and act, are very sexy to women.

Nothing is less attractive to a woman than a guy who walks around on eggshells, who is a pleaser, or who constantly doubts himself. She will constantly test you to see how strong you are.

Be a real man.

9) Own Your Masculine Power. Your masculine strength allows her sexual feminine energy to emerge. Sexual energy and attraction is caused by polarity. This means that, as the man, you must be fully confident and grounded in your masculinity, allowing her to relax into her soft and sensual femininity.

As you are secure in your masculine energy, you will be bold, you will be strong, and the safe foundation on which she can build her trust. This will allow her to surrender to you, and allow you to lead her. She desperately wants to know you are safe. Even the strongest women get tired of being strong all the time. She wants to know that you are strong enough to hold that space for her, so she doesn't have to be . . . and she wants to know that you have the strength to allow her wild, passionate side to be untamed.

10) Sometimes you need to just take her. In the strength of your masculinity sometimes she wants you to just pick her up and carry her to the bedroom as she surrenders to your power. She craves to feel your passion as you pin her against the wall and kiss her. She hungers to feel your raw, primal strength and desire for her. She yearns for you to be strong enough to unlock that deepest part of her soul.

Marriage should be that safe space to unleash all of your passion in the bedroom—and any other crazy place you can think of.

She wants this too, but she needs to feel safe, loved, and cherished first before she allows you into this sacred part of her.

11) Listen to her and focus on her pleasure first. Learn how to be a great lover by asking what she likes, listening to her body, and discovering what turns her on. Experiment and see what each of you likes. There will be certain times where she will want one thing, and other times when she won't. Never force her to do something she doesn't enjoy.

A great lover will try as much as possible to help her have an orgasm before intercourse. This may help her to even have multiple orgasms during sex, and the more she enjoys it, the more she will want to have it.

FOR THE WOMEN:

Here are the things you should know about your man, his need for sex, and how to help him to be the man you want to make love to.

It begins with understanding that for a man, sex is not just a desire, but a core need. It is one of the main things that makes him feel connected and one with you.

1) **Focus on your fulfillment first**. Guys are pretty simple when it comes to how they work. You on the other hand are much more complicated when it comes to sex. When you enjoy yourself, you will find fulfillment and joy in it, and will want it more. When you enjoy it, the man will feel like he is doing a good job, which fills his core need—to feel like a hero. Find ways to make sex deeply enjoyable for you, and it will be a much richer and rewarding experience for both of you.

2) **Tell him what you want**. Tell him what feels good and what turns you on. Let him know when he is doing something right. Make it easy

for him to be a great lover. Be open. Don't expect him to read your mind. Remember his deepest desire is to please you, but he needs your help in knowing how to do that. This may require you taking time to explore and decide what you do like. Be willing to try new things and then communicate about what you want.

3) **Be alluring**. Let that feminine sensual goddess in you be fully alive. This is especially important after you have kids and get consumed with the daily stresses of life.

Work on being attractive. Take good care of yourself. Exercise. Be healthy. Dress up. Wear perfume. Flirt with him. Nurture and allow the sensual, sexy part of you to be fully expressed. Be like a flower whose natural radiance draws him irresistibly toward you.

4) **Never withhold sex**. When he makes an effort to connect with you, don't reject him. Never use it as a way to control or punish him. Make it safe for him to feel like he can be intimate with you.

Many women get frustrated because they feel their man is always wanting sex. Sorry, ladies, but you married a man. Be grateful that you have a man that loves you and is attracted to you. It would be unhealthy if he didn't want to have sex with you. It is his natural way of bonding with you. It's a good thing that he wants to make love to you.

When you say no to a man it is the deepest form of rejection. It devastates his self-esteem and it will make him more hesitant to ask you in the future. It strips him of his masculine strength and if you continue to reject him it will build resentment and he may stop asking altogether. If he feels like he can't get his sexual needs met in the marriage, he will be tempted to fill those needs outside the marriage either through porn or infidelity.

When you say no, what you may be really saying is "I'm tired, I'm stressed and my mind is so full and cluttered that I'm not feeling very sexy right now," but what he HEARS is "I don't love you. I don't respect you. I don't trust you. I don't want you. "

Please understand: I'm *not* saying you have to always say yes, or that you have to have sex if you feel strongly you don't want to. There will be times that you may not be in the mood but you will have sex just because you love him and he is important to you and it is your way of meeting his needs. But if you really don't want to and you have sex only out of obligation, it violates the true intimacy of the relationship, and can create bitterness and negative anchors.

If you don't want to have sex, take time to figure out why, communicate openly with your husband, and work on doing what it takes to create the desire. Maybe it's just that specific moment in time, and if you have more time to prepare it will be fine. Maybe you need him to show up and support you with other things and listen to you. Maybe you have some emotional things you need to work through. Maybe you are experiencing health challenges or problems with your hormones that you need to take care of.

Be proactive in finding ways to meet this important need for your relationship. What can *you* do to prepare yourself, to get excited about having sex, to create sexual desire within yourself? Do you need self-care time, such as taking a bubble bath, shaving your legs, getting a massage, buying new lingerie or putting on some perfume?

Don't wait for your husband to create the right "mood"—take initiative to bring out your powerfully feminine, sexual side. Take time to do something each day that makes you feel feminine and beautiful.

If you haven't had pleasurable sexual experiences before, take ownership and begin today to create the right environment for it. If you're not enjoying sex, ask yourself, "Why not?" And take more ownership in figuring out how to create a powerful sexual experience for both of you.

Clear communication is essential to make sure he can honor where you are at.

If you are "not in the mood," honor yourself by communicating clearly and respectfully what your needs are. Honor him by expressing your desire for him and by actively working to show him your continued commitment to this important and critical part.

For instance, here are some ways to communicate your needs without it damaging your relationship:

"I'd love to honey, but I'm feeling so exhausted right now and really need some rest, would it be okay if we took some time in the morning or tomorrow?"

"Thanks, I love that you want to make love to me. I have so much on my mind right now, maybe if you could take some time to talk to me and help me tidy up, it would help me clear my mind so I would be more in the mood."

"I'm not in the mood for sex right now, but maybe you could just hold me. How about we just take some time to snuggle for a bit?"

5) Untame the sensual Divine feminine Goddess that you are. Marriage should be a safe place for you to fully express yourself, including the wild, playful, sexy side of you. Sometimes you should be the one to initiate sex and seduce your husband. Surprise him in some sexy lingerie. Drag him into the bedroom. Push him onto the bed. Dance for him. Tease him. Light him up. Be creative. Be spontaneous. This is a part of you he wants to see unleashed, and which you are yearning to have freed yourself.

Just as unhealthy patterns around sex can cause a lot of problems in marriage, good, healthy, fulfilling sex can actually *solve* a lot of problems.

Understand that while this is the advice I wish I would have had, and advice that I believe serves many couples, there are many different situations that are unique to each couple.

Take the time to study and communicate what your ideal sexual relationship would look like.

THE PRACTICE:

An assignment to practice sex??? *(I think I can hear the guys cheering here—and hopefully the women too.)*

Yes. But sorry to say this homework begins outside the bedroom. Becoming a great lover requires understanding, good communication, and diligence.

Begin by understanding what you enjoy and would like to experience in your sexual relationship. And then find some time in the next 48 hours where you can have some authentic conversation with your spouse to discuss your desires in your intimate relationship.

Here are some sample questions that might help you to understand each other's needs, desires, turn-ons, and turn-offs….

In an ideal world, how often would you like to have sex?

What are some of your favorite memories of when we've made love?

What are specific things outside of the bedroom that I can do to create emotional intimacy?

What are the things you need to feel to desire sex?

What are specific things I can do that make you feel safe?

What are things that you enjoy most in sex?

What would you like to experience more of/less of?

What time of day or night do you prefer?

(These are just sample questions to get you thinking how you can express more clearly the meaningful intimacy you desire . . . and then after talking about it, feel free to go passionately make love.)

RESOURCES:

I recently went through an incredible audio program that was designed to help couples create more true intimacy in their marriage called *Fuel Her Fire* by Felice Dunas. It had so many insights on intimacy I wish I would've had earlier in my marriage. I highly recommend every man get this.

You can find a link to this course and other books to assist you at www.epic-marriage.com/resources. On that page you will also find a free training call I recorded on the Art of Intimacy.

{ PRINCIPLE THIRTEEN: }

DON'T BE AN IDIOT

> ***DON'T BE AN IDIOT.*** *And don't be afraid of being one either. You will make mistakes and so will she. Try not to make too big of mistakes, and learn from the ones you do make. You're not supposed to be perfect, just try not to be too stupid.*

Life is about making mistakes and learning from them. There is no way around the fact that when you live with someone, they are going to make some stupid mistakes, and you will too.

What you do with those mistakes when they happen is what will determine whether your marriage is strengthened or threatened.

You can't live life in fear of making mistakes, because you will. Sometimes you'll say stupid things, make bad decisions about money, lose control of your emotions, and do things you regret. The sooner you apologize, course correct, and learn the lessons, the better and wiser you will become, and the stronger your relationship will grow.

Have patience with your spouse. They are not perfect, and neither are you.

A major factor in the quality of your marriage is how well you *ask for forgiveness* when you have made mistakes, and how well you *forgive* when the other person makes mistakes. Neither of those is easy, but both are necessary.

The more you give your spouse grace, and learn to forgive their mistakes, the more you can support them in making the changes needed.

Be aware that if you make big mistakes you will have to deal with the consequences for a long time. Abuse, infidelity, affairs, and lying are things which leave deep, deep wounds in a marriage and it may take a long, long time to rebuild trust.

Can you heal a relationship after those huge mistakes? Absolutely, but only if both people are really willing to do the work. But it's best by far if you're just not an idiot and don't do those things to begin with.

THE PRACTICE:

One of the greatest skills you have as a Conscious Creator, someone who takes accountability and control in their life, is the ability to look at mistakes as growing opportunities. Problems and challenges can actually become seeds to sow in the garden of your life, leading to great fruitfulness. Growth requires awareness and humility, though. Take some time to identify your mistakes and discover the gifts that each of them have brought into your life.

Step 1) Draw a line down the center of a piece of paper and on the left-hand column at the top write the word "MISTAKES."

Step 2) Take 5-10 minutes and on the left-hand column make a list of as many of your mistakes and failures as you can remember.

Step 3) Go through the list and next to a mistake write down on the right-hand column what you've learned or gained from that experience.

Step 4) Cross out the word "~~MISTAKES~~" and on the right hand column write the word "VICTORIES."

RESOURCES:

Through my events and the various coaching programs that I offer, I empower individuals and couples to become more powerful and aware Conscious Creators. If you have felt stuck in your life and marriage, and don't know how to create the changes you want in your life, then I invite you to check out the resources and programs we have available to help you.

To learn more about our coaching programs and events to help you grow as an individual and a couple,
visit www.epic-marriage.com/mentoring

{ PRINCIPLE FOURTEEN: }

GIVE HER SPACE

> ***GIVE HER SPACE.*** *The woman is so good at giving and giving, and sometimes she will need to be reminded to take time to nurture herself. Sometimes she will need to fly from your branches to go and find what feeds her soul, and if you give her that space she will come back with new songs to sing (okay, getting a little too poetic here, but you get the point). Tell her to take time for herself,* especially *after you have kids. She needs that space to renew and get re-centered, and to find herself after she gets lost in serving you, the kids, and the world.*

You don't *own* your spouse. Men, you shouldn't try to control your wife. And women, it's not your job to be a mother to your husband.

Giving each other *freedom* and space to be yourselves, to pursue your own interests and passions, and to grow individually is critical for the long-term health of the relationship.

In order for any marriage to be whole and complete, it requires two whole and complete individuals, two individuals who are growing individually and also growing together.

So many marriages struggle because of some level of codependency.

Women, it seems, especially have difficulty in taking time for themselves after they have children. They become used to giving so much to their kids, to their husband, to their work, and to their communities, that in time many feel like they are completely depleted and have nothing left to give to themselves.

MEN: You should encourage your wife to pursue her hobbies, spend time with good friends, and to nurture and pamper herself.

When you do this, you will notice she comes back with so much more to give, and with a renewed sense of passion and energy.

WOMEN: Often your husband will need his "man time": spending time with his guy friends, playing or watching sports, going to a movie, or having personal time in his man-cave. This personal time is when he can collect his thoughts and release the stresses of his work and life. Men, especially when they are dealing with stress, will often want to be alone.

A marriage can only be as healthy as each individual within the marriage. If you are not doing the self-nurturing to take care of yourselves then it's common for one or both spouses to get to a point of depletion and depression.

It's vital that both of you continue to have your own friends, hobbies, and interests—and then to consciously create space in which you come back together to spend time building your relationship and growing together.

When both of you are happy and fulfilled, you have so much more to give back to each other.

THE PRACTICE:

When we spend so much time in a relationship with someone else, we begin to lose sight of those things that we do that can make us feel whole and complete as individuals. When we are so used to sacrificing and giving to everyone else, it's easy to forget how to receive from others and how to nurture ourselves.

By caring for yourself you will find healthy ways to deal with stress, overcome mental and physical exhaustion, and develop a deeper sense of peace, happiness, and well-being.

Much like you did when you created the self-care list in a previous chapter, take a few minutes and brainstorm to create a **Self-Nurturing List** of things you can do when you are feeling tired, stressed, or depleted.

What are ten specific things you can do to take time for yourself, away from your spouse and kids, and fill yourself up?

SELF-NURTURE LIST

(i.e. walking in nature, hot bubble bath, massage, watching a movie, reading a book, going to a yoga or exercise class, going to an art gallery or concert, time spent alone in meditation or prayer, shopping for a new outfit, going to a seminar or workshop on something you enjoy…)

1)____

2)____

3)____

4)____

5)____

6)____

7)____

8)____

9)____

10)_______________________________________

RESOURCES:

During my three-day breakthrough event Live BIG, you will be guided through a process I call "Conscious Lifestyle Design," where you get to really define what it is that makes you feel happy and alive. There you will become clear on what your ideal life looks like in your health, your relationships, and your money, and more importantly, how to begin creating it.

To learn more and to attend Live BIG,
visit www.LiveBigSeminar.com and enter the promo code "BOOKSPECIAL" to receive a 50% discount. To attend for free, become a marriage ambassador and help me on my mission to save 1,000 marriages. www.epic-marriage.com/ambassador

{ PRINCIPLE FIFTEEN: }

BE VULNERABLE

> ***BE VULNERABLE.*** *You don't have to have it all together. Be willing to share your fears and feelings and quick to acknowledge your mistakes.*

Wow. This is a hard one for most of us guys.

To be able to share our feelings, to admit that we're afraid, to ask for help, or to actually cry takes more courage than most of us men have.

I know for me, I always felt like I had it altogether. Admitting I was struggling with something or that I had made a mistake was so hard to do.

Remember, a guy's primary driving need in the relationship is to be the *hero* and to be respected, but somehow in the mind of many men that translates into *I can't reveal that I have any weaknesses.*

The truth is, the only way to create the deepest level of connection with your spouse is to drop the mask when you're pretending to have it all together.

The funny thing is that women are attracted to men who can communicate and be emotionally vulnerable. Women see it as a strength in a man who can be open with his heart and allow for that space of emotional intimacy.

The irony is your woman will trust you *more* when you stop pretending to be perfect.

In order to get to this space of confidence and vulnerability, however, it requires you to have a deep, deep level of unconditional self-love and approval. This means you must be okay with your shadow as well as your light. When you are truly comfortable with yourself, then you will no longer live in fear of rejection from others if you show up authentically.

THE PRACTICE:

Men especially have a hard time recognizing and expressing their emotions such as fear, anxiety, or sadness. Their egos also make it so they don't want to acknowledge their mistakes and weaknesses, even to themselves.

There are times when it's appropriate to work through your emotions on your own, and times when sharing with your spouse can not only give you the support you want, but also deepen the connection and bond in your marriage.

A lot of this practice is just learning to be present and aware of the emotions you are experiencing and learning to acknowledge and express them for yourself.

This is a simple exercise to be done frequently to help you become present at this moment to what you are feeling, and to create awareness of why you are feeling that way.

The following is a list that will help you identify your emotions as you experience them.

The emotion that I'm feeling right now is:

Joy	Relief	Hungry	Certainty
Love	Wonder	Happy	Tired
Sadness	Wonderful	Helpless	Irritated
Anxious	Grief	Hopeful	Dizzy
Afraid	Energetic	Merciful	Longing
Lust	Dread	Lucky	Relaxed
Envy	Empathy	Content	Embarrassed
Rapture	Disgust	Pity	Surprised
Angst	Apathy	Vulnerable	Amused
Gratitude	Sympathy	Guilty	Horrified
Jealous	Sweaty	Hatred	Excited
Confident	Stupid	Sleepy	Annoyed
Compassion	Cold	Anger	Proud
Awe	Ashamed	Bored	

The reason I feel this way is:

RESOURCES:

Learning to be truly comfortable and confident with who we are is one of the greatest rewards in the personal development journey. At Live BIG and the other events and mentoring programs I offer, participants tap into a deeper level of confidence and personal power than they have ever experienced. This will help you to show up more fully and authentically in your relationships and every other area of your life.

To learn more about our coaching programs, Live BIG and other events to help you grow as an individual and a couple visit www.epic-marriage.com/mentoring

{ PRINCIPLE SIXTEEN: }

Be Fully Transparent

Be fully transparent. *If you want to have trust you must be willing to share everything, especially those things you don't want to share. It takes courage to fully love, to fully open your heart, and let her in when you don't know if she will like what she finds. Part of that courage is allowing her to love you completely—your darkness as well as your light. Drop the mask. If you feel like you need to wear a mask around her, and show up perfect all the time, you will never experience the full dimension of what love can be.*

Our fear of transparency and vulnerability shows up in many ways. For me, I grew up always trying to be the "good boy."

I think subconsciously I was always fighting for love and approval from my mom, and so I had to get good grades, keep my room clean, and be the peacemaker.

When I got married, this same pattern and addiction to making it look like I had it all together continued.

Because I was so afraid of being rejected or not being accepted, I couldn't acknowledge it when I was struggling, or admit the mistakes I had made, or let on that I didn't have the answers.

So I put on this mask that I wore day in and day out, projecting to the world that I didn't have any problems.

When we wear a mask, it prevents us from truly receiving love and approval of others, because we discount it by thinking, *They don't really love me. They love this mask I am wearing. If they really knew me they wouldn't say that.*

Ultimately, when we are afraid of being transparent and authentic, we rob ourselves of the opportunity to get help and grow together. Worst of all, it creates *distrust* in the relationship, because the other person subconsciously detects that we are hiding something.

In the deeply intimate experience of marriage, attempts to hide *anything* will violate that trust and connection.

So how do you become a transparent, authentic spouse?

First, please refer to Principle 13 and **don't be an idiot**, so you don't have major mistakes to hide.

And second, when you do mess up, realize that trying to hide it doesn't fix what you've done, it amplifies the problem. Be honest with yourself and honest with your spouse, and your trust in each other will miraculously grow.

If the goal is *true intimacy*, then you must learn to show up fully and authentically, without the mask and without anything to hide.

Learning to love ourselves completely is the most important work we will ever do to create a thriving marriage and life.

THE PRACTICE:

I don't believe that you should share *everything* that happens in your life or share *all* of your thoughts with your spouse. That would be overwhelming and counterproductive. She doesn't need to know what time you brushed your teeth or what type of donut you ate at work.

True transparency is about opening up your heart and having the level of trust where nothing needs to be kept a secret, and you don't feel the need to hide any part of who you are from your spouse.

True intimacy requires us to show up fully, vulnerably, without the mask, and to trust our partner will love us, shadow and all.

The only way for us to show up fully and authentically, and expect someone else to love us, is to love and accept ourselves fully first.

Learning to *love ourselves* completely is the most important work we will ever do to create a thriving marriage and life.

This can be hard work. And it may take time. Be patient with yourself.

Visit www.epic-marriage.com/resources to download and listen to the free bonus audio: "Shadow and Sacred Self-Meditation."

RESOURCES:

In addition to downloading and listening to the bonus audio, "Shadow and Sacred Self-Meditation," I recommend you read *The Dark Side of the Light Chasers* by Debbie Ford. It is one of the most powerful books I've read, and the processes in that book helped me so much to overcome my fears and learn to love myself unconditionally. When that happened it became easy for me to be free and authentic with those around me.

To download the bonuses, see other book recommendations, and find other resources to support you, visit www.epic-marriage.com/resources

{ PRINCIPLE SEVENTEEN: }

NEVER STOP GROWING TOGETHER

> ***NEVER STOP GROWING TOGETHER.*** *The stagnant pond breeds malaria, the flowing stream is always fresh and cool. Atrophy is the natural process when you stop working a muscle, just as it is if you stop working on your relationship. Find common goals, dreams, and visions to work toward.*

LIFE.

Have you thought about what this word means? What's the difference between something that is alive versus dead?

Life is about growth, learning, and expansion.

Marriage can be one of the greatest catalysts in our life for growth.

I had a teacher who would often say, "If you're not busy growing, you're busy dying."

I think about that a lot as it relates to marriage and creating a thriving relationship. If you stop nurturing the plant in the garden, the plant will begin to wither. The same is true in your relationship.

"Change," it's said, "is the only constant." Growth, however, is a choice.

There are many who go through change only to remain committed to being the same, and when we don't learn from history we are doomed to repeat it.

Or, as Eric Hoffer states so eloquently, *"In seasons of change the learners will inherit the earth, while the learned will find themselves beautifully equipped to deal with a world that no longer exists."*

The truth is, change will come whether you want it to or not.

Throughout your marriage, you will move, have kids, change jobs, get ill, grow gray and wrinkled, have monumental victories and major defeats.

Everything in your life will be different over time.

But there is a huge difference between *conscious change* and unconscious or accidental change.

Being a Conscious Creator in your marriage requires you to have a vision for where you are going and where you want to go, what you want to have, and what you want to accomplish as a couple.

Imagine this: You decide you want to go on a trip, so you hop in the car and just start driving. You haven't decided where you want to go, so you turn left here, and right there, whenever you feel like it. Sometimes you just decide to follow the person in front of you, because they act like they know where they're going. You go down whatever roads you end up on until you can go no further.

Imagine if you kept driving like this; where do you think you would end up?

Most likely you'd run out of gas, in some desert, slum, dead end or somewhere you don't want to be.

But that would be crazy, right? No one would ever do this in a car, but people do this *all the time* in their relationships and in life!

They just jump in and go with the flow on a daily basis, doing whatever feels right or convenient at the moment, following the people around them, and then are surprised when they find themselves at a dead end, wondering how they got there.

I've often heard experts say that the average person will spend more time planning a vacation to Disneyland than they do setting goals and planning their life.

What if you actually approached your relationships with the same seriousness you do in planning a vacation? You decide where you want to go, set some goals of how long you want to take, and then, as you make the drive, every decision is based on how to get to that destination. If you get off course, you simply turn around, make some adjustments, and keep on driving till you get there.

When a couple has this vision, and both of you are actively working to grow in your marriage, then progressing through the different phases and challenges of life can be a wonderful adventure.

When you and your spouse lack unified vision for your marriage, you end up feeling like you're on opposing teams, getting lost in the unimportant little challenges in life.

The only way to have a successful marriage long-term is to work and live as though you are on the same team, consciously work toward your goals, embrace the changes that come into your lives, and move together through the challenges that stand in your way.

Throughout your relationship, you will grow through many stages of love. Each of these stages requires a conscious choice to either grow together through the changes life brings, or drift apart.

THE FOUR STAGES OF LOVE

Stage 1) **ROMANTIC LOVE**: This is the season of new love. It is filled with infatuation, excitement, and euphoria. This is when sexual attraction is off the charts and both partners are actively investing and showing off their best side as they court each other.

When you fall in love, your brain releases a cocktail of chemicals *(including oxytocin, phenylethylamine, and dopamine)* designed to set your heart thumping and, of course, light a fire in your loins.

This season is filled with hope, desire, attraction, and dreams of "happily ever after."

This stage is the springtime of love, filled with growth and possibility, where you're planting your garden for the first time and anything is possible.

During this stage it is important to create as many good habits in your relationship as possible. Enjoy the exciting connection and create as many memories as possible before your life gets swept away with the responsibilities of kids and life. Be conscious of what it is that you do when you are courting and romancing your loved one, then discover how to keep that fire lit.

This stage will typically last between six months and two years.

Stage 2) **REALISTIC LOVE**: After the sparks fade, you are left with the reality of building a life with someone who is very different from you. At first you were attracted to those differences, but now they start to drive you crazy. In this stage, you become acutely aware of all your spouse's shortcomings and have a laundry list of things you would like them to change. There is a growing list of disappointments, as you deal with the stresses of everyday life, managing kids and money, and lots of ups and downs.

During this stage, the emotional high of new romantic love fades and you realize that *love is a choice* and one that you have to make every day, otherwise the weeds will take over your garden. You realize that in order for this marriage to work, *you* are going to need to work. The work involves learning and practicing the skills of unconditional love, intimacy, communication, forgiveness, and nurturing your loved one's love language.

Stage 3) **RESTLESS LOVE**: There comes a point in life and relationships when you wonder if all the work is worth it or if the grass really is greener on the other side. In can come as part of a midlife crisis, or after a long season of unhappiness in your marriage. It's easy to fall prey to the fantasy of life being easier if you were alone or with someone else.

When you let your guard down, you become a prime candidate for an affair, whether real or imagined, physical or emotional, because you've allowed yourself to believe that there is someone else out there better suited to be your soul mate and give you everything you feel you are missing in your relationship right now.

This stage will give you another opportunity to really commit wholeheartedly to your marriage.

It is so tempting to throw away everything you have built, but you need to make a commitment to stay the course. It is vital that you also *find yourself* again. A lot of your dissatisfaction arises when you have lost yourself in the relationship. These restless feelings are urgings from within for you to find yourself, and in doing so you will rediscover your partner along the way.

Continuing to recommit to work on yourself, and to work on the relationship through this stage is the only way to get to the ultimate goal you are seeking: rewarding love.

Stage 4) **REWARDING LOVE**: This is the enduring love that only comes after forging through the great challenges of life together and realizing that, despite all of their faults, this spouse of yours is the one that you want to have by your side for the rest of your life.

Your spouse has seen you at your worst and is still there by your side. And that says a lot. You have learned to forgive each other fully, to give each other space and freedom, and to work together using each of your own strengths.

At this stage of love, you have found a way to support and nurture each other and to find happiness for yourself. You have discovered the power of working as a team, and you're both excited about the future. There is a deep trust that has grown, not because either of you are perfect, but because you have learned to love each other in spite of your imperfections.

All the years of planting, watering, and nurturing your relationship have finally allowed the roots to go deep and strong, and the plant is yielding the delicious fruit you've always desired.

During this stage, just like with every other, it's important to continue to grow together and continually nurture what you have.

There are no defined time frames for how long each of these stages last for couples. Some grow through the stages and find themselves at rewarding love quickly, while some can be married their entire life and never grow to have the rewarding love they desire.

If we go by divorce statistics though, it's clear that a lot of couples give up before they reach rewarding love. If rewarding love is the goal, you must be willing to graduate through each of the stages and choose to commit and love through them all.

What's important is to constantly choose to grow, both as an individual and as a couple.

Have a clear vision for what you want, commit to work on creating it daily, learn from your mistakes, and get a little bit better every day.

This is how you will discover the growth that is possible when your relationship is fully *alive*.

THE PRACTICE:

Having worthwhile goals as a couple is critical. It's when we are heading in different directions that we lose intimacy and connection.

Take a date as a couple where you can dream and define some areas that you want to grow and improve and some of the long and short-term goals you want to work toward.

Use these questions to get your mind thinking about your goals. (These are specifically goals you can work together on as a couple, though you should have personal goals too.)

Visit www.epic-marriage.com/resources. Download and listen to the bonus audio: "The Couple's Goal Workshop."

Answer these questions as a couple:

Looking SIX MONTHS into the future . . .

What are the things you love about your life now that you want to keep the same?

What are the changes you want to experience in your health in the next six months?

What are the specific changes you want to see in your relationship in the next six months?

Are there places you'd like to travel to for vacation?

What are some fun experiences you'd like to have?

Are there things you'd like to save up to buy?

Are there specific things you'd like to learn as a couple?

Are there classes or seminars you could attend together?

What dreams do you have that you can start working toward?

Now take just one of these areas at a time and ask:

Who do I need to have support from to make this happen?

What exactly is the goal that I am committing to?

When do I want to have this happen?

Why is this important to me?

How do I make this a reality?

What changes in my personal life do I need to make in order to achieve this goal?

Then break the goal into simple steps, so you know what you can take action on today. Next, answer this:

*What is **one** small thing you can do **right now** to make progress toward your goal?*

RESOURCES:

Be sure to download the free bonus audio on Goal Setting I have provided for you at www.epic-marriage.com/resources For more in-depth support, I have several courses, seminars, and coaching programs that will help you discover your purpose and set and achieve your goals. You can also read my blog for some free training.

For more information about these programs as well as other free information on how to Live BIG visit www.geraldrogers.com

{ PRINCIPLE EIGHTEEN: }

DON'T WORRY ABOUT MONEY

> ***DON'T WORRY ABOUT MONEY.*** *Money is a game. Find ways to work together as a team to win it. It never helps when teammates fight. Figure out ways to leverage both persons' strengths to win.*

Money is one of my favorite topics to coach individuals and couples on, because, like sex, it is one that creates so much synergy and happiness when it's working, and so much frustration and problems when it's not.

I feel like I've been very blessed financially, but managing my finances has not always been an easy thing for me. Sometimes it has been incredibly painful, stressful, and frustrating.

I have always been self-employed, from being a freelance illustrator, to starting a real-estate investing company, to launching my consulting and speaking business. With that, I put my wife and family through years of up-and-down roller-coaster income, as I tried to get my businesses running.

After five years of building my real estate company in Orlando, Florida, my business hit a devastating challenge with the collapse of the real estate market.

I remember clearly one night in 2008, when I was up late staring at a stack of unopened bills on my desk. My eyes were bloodshot red from tears and several sleepless nights. I had no idea how I was going to pay those bills and provide for my family.

That evening I finally had the hard conversation I had always feared. I confessed to my wife where we were really at financially, and that we had to declare bankruptcy. I had to tell her that all my dreams and efforts to make us financially free by investing in real estate had made us broke, and now, after the market had crashed, I was deep in debt with eight properties in foreclosure.

I had no idea how to pay the mortgage on our own house, much less how to buy food and all the other needs of my young family.

I remember how the stress of our marriage was compounded because we were so ineffective at talking and working as a team on our finances. My wife and I had two totally different money personalities, and my approach had become to just not talk to her about my business money, give her a check each month, and let her figure out and manage all the household budgeting.

The more we avoided working together, the deeper the challenges got financially and emotionally.

If you're like most couples, you've probably struggled with money in your marriage. For most people, the issue of finances is one of the biggest challenges that they face in their marriage.

While it should be a tool to help a couple create the lifestyle they desire, too often it becomes a source of stress, arguments, and frustration.

When you come into a relationship, you both come with your own baggage of beliefs and habits about money, what it means, and how to spend it. Most likely the person you were attracted to has some very different ideas about money than you.

This is a good thing. I repeat: It's a **good thing** that your spouse doesn't think about money exactly like you!

Why? Because just like being on any team, you want each member of the team to bring his or her own strengths, experience, perspective, and values to the game.

I love the quote that says, *"If both people in a relationship always thought the same, then one of them would be unnecessary."*

I should clarify that it is a good thing *only* if you are choosing to work together as a team in reaching your goals. This requires that you have a common vision and goal, you respect each other's strengths, and that each person is actively working to reach these goals and support their teammate.

Couples who have an unhealthy attitude about money resent the way their partner handles it, keep secrets from each other, or avoid dealing with it altogether.

In the end, these couples, instead of working together to win the money game, end up fighting, disrespecting each other, and playing to lose.

If you were an observer looking at the way you and your spouse have been playing this game of money, what would you see?

Do you actively take time to work together and discuss money or do you avoid talking about it?

Do you have clearly defined financial goals that you are actively working toward as a couple for this year and for retirement? Or are you pretty much just winging it and hoping it works out?

Do you understand and respect your teammate's strengths and views about money? Or are you resentful about the way they deal with it?

Here's **THE MONEY ADVICE I WISH I WOULD'VE HAD.**

1) Make money important, and commit to being good at the money game.

Many people struggle with money because they don't make it a priority to be good at earning, managing, and investing it. Anyone can learn to be great at money management, but they need to make it a priority first.

A lot of people grew up with a limiting belief, a subconscious *scarcity mindset* that said, "Money doesn't grow on trees. There's never enough money. I don't deserve to be rich. Rich people are greedy. Money is the root of all evil. You can't be spiritual and rich. Money isn't important."

These internal beliefs will dictate how you earn, spend, and save money. In essence they define your "money blueprint," and the amount of money you create and keep in life. It will also affect how you and your spouse deal with money matters.

Take the time to figure out what your true negative beliefs are about money, and then begin the work of shifting those to more empowering beliefs. And then make it a priority to become *financially educated.*

2) Create clearly defined goals with a realistic plan.

Before you start running, decide where you are trying to go. Before you start laying bricks, decide what it is that you are building.

What is your retirement goal? How much money will you need? How much should you be saving monthly? How are you going to get that money to work for you? What are family vacations or upcoming events you need to save for? What is your goal for an emergency fund? How much do you need for that new home, car, or trip?

Get clarity and then start building.

3) Pay yourself first.

This is non-negotiable, *especially* if you feel like you can't afford to.

Take the very first 10 percent of everything you earn and put it away into long-term savings or investments where it can work for you.

If you wait until everything else has been paid before you pay yourself, you will never have enough. But in some strange, magical way, if you pay yourself first, then you'll find a way to take care of everything else with the remaining funds.

4) Build a "dream team" with professionals who are smarter than you.

If you want to win this game of money, surround yourself with people who can help you that are great at what they do.

Hire tax professionals who can make sure you pay as little as legally possible to the government.

Hire financial advisors who are great at finding ways to make your money work for you rather than against you.

Hire attorneys who can help make sure you protect your assets and make sure you have a will, trust, and other things in place so you are prepared for the future.

5) Have regular "Money Masterminds."

This is where you sit down as a couple, free from distractions, and talk to each other about your goals, where you're at, and what you can do better.

It is critical as a team that you talk openly about money and your desires and concerns. During these masterminds, you should get clear on your assets, monthly expenses, ideas to make and save more money, upcoming financial needs, and how you can support each other better.

There must be **no money secrets** in the relationship.

These masterminds should be put in the calendar either on a weekly or monthly basis. Sometimes these should be done with other players on your team, including financial advisors, tax professionals, or other money mentors.

6) Avoid the debt trap. And if you're in it, get out as soon as you can.

Create clear guidelines as to what you will use credit for and what you won't. Outside of your home, car, education, and wealth-creating assets, avoid debt like the plague.

Realize that if you buy consumer goods like TVs, furniture, vacations, toys and food with credit, and pay it off at the minimum each month you will pay two to three times as much as its worth. So don't. Pay cash for those things.

And most importantly: If you can't afford it, *don't buy it.* (I know, novel concept.)

If you are caught in a debt trap already, create a "freedom plan" to get out of debt and stay out forever.

7) Invest wisely. Never invest in something you don't understand.

Making your money work for you is the goal of every investment. To turn your hard-earned dollars into little workers that are making money for you twenty-four hours a day without you and bringing in a good return is the goal of the wise investor. Take the time to study and understand every investment before investing. There is no such thing as truly passive income. Every investment requires ongoing care and management

Avoid the temptation to speculate and invest in businesses, stocks, real estate and other opportunities that you don't really understand, regardless of the promises others make. It's incredibly easy to lose money when you don't understand what you're investing in.

8) Have personal play money.

It's important as a couple you share your assets and resources, but it's also important that you have some personal freedom too. Whether it's fifty dollars or five hundred, find an amount that works for you to be free to spend however you want.

By budgeting some personal play money for both husband and wife, it gives you a sense of independence where you can spend it on whatever feels good to you, without the spouse feeling bitter.

For spender personalities, this is vital in order to have that feeling of freedom. For savers, it is important to actually spend the money, even if your tendency is to save it.

Having "freedom money" that you can spend on whatever you want nurtures a sense of abundance and fulfillment. And if you feel guilty when spending money on yourself, then it can help you remember that you are worth it.

9) Invest in yourself.

Of all the things that you can invest in, your most valuable asset is the six inches between your ears.

Be a lifelong student, and continually seek education that will help you win this money game. Get audiobooks to listen to in the car, attend seminars, get higher education, hire a coach, and talk to people who know more than you do.

Be curious.

Enhance your skills and expertise in your work so that you can get paid more. Commit to being world class at what you do, and stay ahead of the curve with your education.

Get financially educated and learn how money works, so that you can save more, and have that money work for you even while you sleep.

Be a *learner* and *take action* on what you discover.

10) Put your relationship before money.

The reality is you *will* have money problems at some point in your marriage. How you deal with those challenges as a couple will determine if they bring you closer together or drive you further apart.

No matter what you go through, always put your relationship before your money.

There will be times you have to be patient, times you need to forgive for mistakes, and times you need to overlook weaknesses in the way your husband or wife deals with money.

Remember, your spouse is more important than money. Treat them that way.

11) And finally . . . have fun.

Since money's a game, choose to play in a way that's fun.

I believe that you should be passionate about everything in your life, including your work. There's nothing more fulfilling than to get paid well while living your purpose.

Yes, you can do what you love *and* get paid well for it.

Rather than living with the mentality that you have to work hard for forty years and then retire so you can finally do what you want, I believe you should do what you want for a living, and sprinkle "mini-retirements" throughout your life, where you get to travel, explore, and celebrate being alive. Have fun winning the game of money!

Money is simply a tool for creating the life that you want. That's it. So design a life worth living and create the resources to live it.

Having money isn't everything, but it can make a lot of things a lot easier.

At the end of the day, if you want to have more money in your life, it comes down to just two things: increasing your skills so you can learn to make more, and being a better steward of the resources you have and learning to save and invest what you have earned.

You should have a plan for both.

As a couple you can easily win this game if you choose. So choose to win it and start working together as a team.

Design a life worth living and create the resources to live it.

THE PRACTICE:

Progress can be made in your financial situation when there is authentic communication about your ideas, fears, and desires about money.

Take time to answer these questions:

What was the money situation for you growing up?

What is the primary "money personality" of you and your spouse? Choose one of the following:

- ***I am a SAVER***: I love to be frugal, spend as little as possible, always look for bargains, and only spend when necessary. I would prefer to put money away for the future than to spend it. This makes me feel safe.

- ***I am a SPENDER***: Money is meant to be enjoyed and I don't worry about it. If I want something, than why shouldn't I have it? I enjoy spending it on both things and experiences. I am less concerned about the future as I am enjoying the present (by the way, I hate budgets).

- ***I am an INVESTOR***: I love to be wise with my money and to make it work for me. It makes me feel successful to see my money grow, and I am always open to new ideas and new opportunities to invest in. I am willing to take risks if I see good potential.

- ***I am an AVOIDER***: I don't like to think about, worry about, or deal with money. I trust that it will all work out, but I don't think it's all that important. I am not that concerned with making a lot of money or with saving it. I believe in a perfect world I wouldn't ever have to worry about money.

How do the money personalities of you and your spouse affect your relationship?

What are the strengths that each of you bring to the table in regards to money?

As a team, what are the financial goals you want to work toward in the next 6 months?

Brainstorm how you can work as a team to achieve this:

RESOURCES:

Download and listen to a ***free*** **bonus audio training** I created on "How to Make More Money While Living Your Purpose." Visit www.epic-marriage.com/resources

{ PRINCIPLE NINETEEN: }

FORGIVE IMMEDIATELY

***FORGIVE IMMEDIATELY**, and focus on the future rather than carrying weight from the past. Don't let your history hold you hostage. Holding on to past mistakes that either you or she makes is like a heavy anchor to your marriage and will hold you back. **Forgiveness is freedom**. Cut the anchor loose and always choose love.*

"A healthy marriage consists of two really good forgivers." -Anonymous

We all have made mistakes, and if you have been married for very long you have all the reasons you need to justify getting a divorce.

But the choice to create an EPIC marriage requires us to let go of the past, again and again and again.

Forgiving doesn't mean *forgetting.*

It means *loving* and *learning.*

Having unconditional love and being completely forgiving doesn't mean that you should be a doormat or allow broken or abusive patterns to recur.

Forgiveness means allowing the past to be in the past and not carrying it forward into the future like a heavy anchor that holds you down, or a toxin that continues to poison your relationship.

But you should learn from past mistakes and make course corrections to ensure they don't happen again in the future.

Remember: *forgiveness* is for *you* as the forgiver.

Forgiveness is what sets *you* free.

When you hold on to bitterness, judgment, or anger, it is a toxin that poisons and punishes *you*. Those are *your emotions* and you are fully accountable for them. They will continue to hold you hostage and hurt you until you choose to *let them go.*

Forgiveness is a *choice* and it is the only path to freedom, regardless of how much you've been hurt, wronged, or taken advantage of.

Your ability to forgive isn't based on the other person apologizing or even asking for forgiveness.

But forgiving doesn't mean you have to allow yourself to be put into a position where you get hurt over and over again. Set healthy boundaries, choose to protect yourself, respect yourself and the other person enough to speak your standards clearly, know where to draw the line, and be willing to remove yourself from relationships where the other person isn't able or willing to act in healthy ways.

And then remember that we all make mistakes and fall short sometimes. Allow the other person to be human just as you are.

And be willing to *forgive yourself*, too.

Forgiveness is for you as the forgiver. Forgiveness sets you free.

THE PRACTICE:

Often it takes a lot of work and patience to fully forgive someone who has hurt us. It requires us to come back to love over and over again. In marriage, your partner will give you hundreds—if not thousands—of opportunities to practice this. Just remember, if you want to experience true intimacy in your relationship, it is YOUR responsibility to learn to forgive and to move on.

Here's a simple process to work on forgiveness. Do this work for anything that you need to forgive your spouse for. This process is not just for spouses, but for anyone towards whom you are holding onto anger or judgment:

What is that someone did or said that you are still resenting or judging them for?

How long have you been carrying this weight, and what has it been costing you?

How long do you want to continue carrying this weight?

Are you ready to let go?

If so, this is how:

1) **See your spouse through God's eyes**. They are a son or daughter of God. Regardless of what choices they have made, they are still worthy of love because of who they are.

God loves them. Leave the judgment up to Him. It's not your job. Your job is to love, not judge.

Picture them in your mind and repeat, "*I honor and love the divine in you.*"

2) **Try to understand and see through *their eyes.*** Realize that what they did to hurt you is due to their own problems and limiting beliefs. It's not about you. Everyone does the best they can with where they are. Remember: *Hurt people hurt people.* See the pain that caused them to act unconsciously and hurt you. Have compassion for them.

   And as you imagine them, say, "*I give you permission to be human.*"

3) **And finally, let the pain go**. Realize you don't need to make their pain your pain. Set yourself free.

   While you imagine them, repeat this: **"I understand. I'm sorry. I forgive you. I love you."** And as you say it, picture the darkness of unforgiveness being released from your body and being replaced with love and light.

   (Sometimes, I need to repeat this dozens of times before I feel my resentment fade and I am fully free of judgment or anger.)

   If you want to have a conversation with them and tell them you forgive them, that's your choice, but it's not required. It may help heal that relationship, but you forgiving alone will release the weight you are carrying.

Forgive freely, over and over again, while learning from the past and making the changes necessary so you don't keep getting hurt.

My invitation is that regardless of how you've been hurt, **always choose love**. This is the only path to peace.

RESOURCES:

The journey of marriage constantly brings us opportunities to forgive, to grow together, and to heal. To help couples through this healing journey and to guide them to a deeper space of love, connection, and intimacy in marriage we have created a 90-day Marriage Mastery course.

To apply to join our next program visit www.epic-marriage.com/mentoring for details.

{ PRINCIPLE TWENTY: }

ALWAYS CHOOSE LOVE

> ***ALWAYS CHOOSE LOVE.*** *Always choose love. Always choose love. In the end, this is the only advice you need. If this is the guiding principle by which all your choices are governed, there is nothing that will threaten the happiness of your marriage. Love will always endure.*

As you plant this garden of love, and continue to grow your marriage, you will constantly be confronted with choices.

There will be times when you will get upset, and times you will be frustrated. There will be moments when you will want to run away and others when you will want to fight.

In every situation you face, you will have a choice as to whether or not to act from selfishness or from love. And each of those choices will impact your future.

In these daily choices, let this one simple question guide you:

What would LOVE do?

I believe this one guiding question will always lead you to do those things in your marriage that will nurture it and bring more happiness and fulfillment.

What would love do, day by day, to express kindness and appreciation to your spouse?

What would love do when your partner is sick and needs support?

What would love do when they are angry or depressed?

Sometimes we're fed this fairy tale and romance novel illusion of what marriage should look like. It was never meant to be "happily ever after." Marriage is like the rest of life, an ever-changing journey with constant opportunities to grow. There will be ups and downs, good times and bad, triumphs and trials.

The greatest beauty of marriage is having a friend and partner on whom you can lean, someone you deeply trust, someone who is willing to make that journey with you.

When LOVE becomes the guiding beacon to all of your decisions, the only possibility is for you to have an EPIC marriage.

FINAL THOUGHTS

As I sit here now, writing the final pages of this book, I'm looking out the windows at the mountain by my home. It was almost a year ago exactly that I sat in this same place, late at night, and wrote the original post that went viral.

And as I sit here, I think of you. In my mind I see you sitting in your home, or wherever you may be reading these words now. And my heart pours out to you.

While I wrote these pages as advice to myself, how I hope that somehow these words that I've shared have touched you in some way. I hope that you have found some meaning and direction to help you in your life and your relationship. I hope that you have found some inspiration and direction to keep moving forward with your marriage, and that some of the tools that I have shared have helped you.

The tears are streaming down my face right now as I think of you and your family.

You deserve to have a happy marriage. Your kids deserve to have two happy parents who are in love and committed to each other. And I believe that wherever you have been and wherever you are at this moment, you and your spouse can commit to create that type of relationship.

There are so many couples right now that struggle in pain, and linger in unhappiness or on the brink of divorce. They're seeking, like I was, for hope and advice that will help them turn their marriage around. I pray that, if this is you, you might find the strength and the wisdom to carry on.

God has led me on an unexpected journey since my divorce.

I never intended to become a relationship expert. After watching my sixteen year marriage crumble, I felt like the least qualified person to teach others how to have a great relationship. But God had different plans. He somehow sees a bigger picture than we do. And as hundreds, and then thousands of people came to me, seeking advice and inspiration on relationships, I began to understand that the pain that I went through and the lessons I learned were the gift that I got to share with the world. My mess had become my message.

And so I've committed to this purpose of working to save over 1,000 marriages from divorce, and to empower and strengthen countless more. To me, it's not just the individuals and the couples, but also the children and the generations to come that I am interested in helping.

To do this I am committed to sharing this message in every way I can.

One of the ways that I believe people are most profoundly impacted, is by being involved with coaching or mentoring programs. This is why I have created a 90-day Marriage Mastery Challenge for anyone who wants support to transform their relationship into the EPIC marriage they want.

If it would serve you and your spouse to create a healthier and more fulfilling relationship, I would be honored to support you on this journey.

Please visit www.epic-marriage.com for details.

I have also created a wealth of other free content and resources to guide people through this journey that you can access at any time at no charge.

Every year, there are millions of people in the U.S. whose marriages end in divorce. I don't pretend to believe that we can save all of them, but we can save some, beginning with a goal of 1,000.

I'm willing to do my part to make this happen, but I know I can't do this alone.

This is where I ask for your help.

First, I ask you to become part of our community, join the conversation, share your story and continue this journey with us as you apply these principles and create transformation in your own life.

Second, I ask you to consider the people in your life that you know who are married who need to hear this message and receive this advice as well. You might be the only one who can reach them.

Will you consider being part of our Marriage Ambassador team, and join us in this mission to save families? It's simple, and you can make a huge difference.

If so, please visit www.epic-marriage.com/ambassador

The divorce statistics are appalling, and something must be done.

Together we can lead a revolution in relationships in this country. We can do this. I know we can. It begins with our own hearts and within the walls of our own homes.

With LOVE and LIGHT, your brother,

Gerald Rogers